"*The Stress Solution* is an unusually wise and well-informed look at the terrible epidemic of stress that hurts so many of us in so many ways. What's more, Dr. Ciaramicoli offers something really new here — pioneering, in fact. If you've struggled with the effects of stress, this is the book for you. I recommend it wholeheartedly."

— **Mira Kirshenbaum**, author of *I Love You but I Don't Trust You:*
The Complete Guide to Restoring Trust in Your Relationship

"This book is a wonderful contribution to the ever-changing field of therapy. Based on research evidence, Dr. Ciaramicoli integrates the science and practice of empathy with traditional cognitive behavioral therapy (CBT) to offer a wise and inspiring solution to the problems associated with stress. This book engages us in easy and effective strategies to help reduce unhelpful ways of thinking and to let go of stress. If you experience stress and are looking for a gentle, practical, and effective solution, empathic CBT will not fail to assist you."

— **Dr. Bruno A. Cayoun**, clinical psychologist,
director of the MiCBT Institute, and author of
Mindfulness-integrated CBT for Well-being and Personal Growth

"Dr. Ciaramicoli has written an insightful and instructional book on empathic CBT. It was a beautiful and growth-inspiring journey for me, and it offers many takeaways and fresh insights. I especially love how, in the final two chapters, Dr. Ciaramicoli weaves all the concepts (i.e., courage, freedom, wisdom, authenticity, and altruism) together almost poetically, all of them mutually reinforcing and each of them enhanced by the power of empathy. Dr. C makes a very strong case for the supposition that empathy is truth-oriented. I couldn't agree more, and this connection is made in our culture so uncommonly that the notion almost seems radical. He also makes the same case for self-knowing and our own growth and development. Just wonderful. I love this book."

— **Dr. James Brennan**, visiting professor of organizational behavior at
Lehigh University and author of *The Art of Becoming Oneself*

"In my many years as a practicing OB/GYN and CEO, I have never seen as many of my female patients negatively affected by stress as I have recently. Not only is Dr. Ciaramicoli's book of wisdom timely, but his way of using empathy to uncover distorted thinking and using CBT techniques to alter these distortions is unique. In addition to being innovative, *The Stress Solution* gives us a practical way to lessen stress and consistently improve overall health. This book will be in my waiting room for a very long time, and I will recommend it to all my patients, colleagues, family, and friends."

— **Mary Bethony, MD**, CEO of All About Women,
Framingham and Westboro, Massachusetts

"Dr. Ciaramicoli has created a new, incredibly effective way to combat stress by combining the use of empathy with the concepts of cognitive behavioral therapy. This book is an excellent tool for combating the stress and anxiety in our current society, and it also teaches us how to balance our lives given the tremendous stressors in our world. I particularly value Dr. C's chapter on the stress of prejudice, which offers a very insightful look at the negative effects of bias and how to perceive free of past conditioning. I have asked my family, friends, and clients to read this wonderful book, and I hope you will do the same for all those you care about."

— **Dr. Robert Cherney**, chief psychologist at Advocates Community
Health Services, Framingham, Massachusetts

"Dr. Ciaramicoli's latest work, *The Stress Solution*, is a must-read. Period. Full stop. In my work as a cognitive behavioral psychologist, I know the power of CBT for managing stress. In my work in the humanitarian sphere, I know the power of empathy. But never before have I seen the two brought together in such a creative and compelling, synergistic approach. How brilliant — logic and emotion combined to augment each other. Bravo, Dr. Ciaramicoli!"

— **Chris Stout, PhD**, founding director of the Center for
Global Initiatives and clinical professor at University of Illinois at
Chicago College of Medicine, Department of Psychiatry

The
Stress
Solution

The
Stress
Solution

Using Empathy and
Cognitive Behavioral Therapy
to Reduce Anxiety and
Develop Resilience

ARTHUR P. CIARAMICOLI, EdD, PhD

New World Library
Novato, California

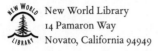

New World Library
14 Pamaron Way
Novato, California 94949

Text design by Megan Colman

Library of Congress Cataloging-in-Publication Data
Names: Ciaramicoli, Arthur P., author.
Title: The stress solution : using empathy and cognitive behavioral therapy to reduce
   anxiety and develop resilience / Arthur P. Ciaramicoli, EdD, PhD.
Description: Novato, California : New World Library, [2016]
Identifiers: LCCN 2016006211 | ISBN 9781608684083 (paperback)
Subjects: LCSH: Stress management. | Empathy. | Cognitive therapy. | BISAC:
   SELF-HELP / Stress Management. | SELF-HELP / Personal Growth / General. |
   PSYCHOLOGY / Psychotherapy / Counseling.
Classification: LCC RA785 .C53 2016 | DDC 616.89/1425—dc23
LC record available at https://lccn.loc.gov/2016006211

First printing, June 2016
ISBN 978-1-60868-408-3
Ebook ISBN 978-1-60868-409-0
Printed in Canada on 100% postconsumer-waste recycled paper

New World Library is proud to be a Gold Certified Environmentally Responsi-ble Publisher. Publisher certification awarded by Green Press Initiative.
www.greenpressinitiative.org

10   9   8   7   6   5   4   3   2   1

To Carmela:
Whenever you are present, the stressors of the world disappear.

Contents

Introduction

Only the development of compassion and understanding for others can
bring us the tranquility and happiness we all seek.

DALAI LAMA XIV, *The Art of Happiness*

A few weekends ago, I was cycling with a good friend, Rob, who
is in excellent physical health, has a good job, loves his wife
and two daughters, and is a wonderful friend. I always look forward
to our long bike rides. As we pedaled and talked, I noted that something was different. As Rob talked about his life, catching me up on
the kids' activities, his wife's upcoming knee surgery, the new roof
he has to pay for, and the college savings he doesn't have, he mentioned the word *stress* in what seemed like every third sentence. Yet
Rob seemed to have little awareness of how often he was mentioning
stress as a part of his life.

I listened to his concerns as we rode along and tried to impart
my understanding. We continued up a difficult hill, where we usually
don't have a lot of breath for talking. However, he continued, with
even more emphasis, "What's wrong with our society that everything seems so important, that we can't slow down for ten minutes,

take a break, and relax? I feel like I'm riding a horse I can't control. I'm holding the reins, but I'm being led instead of leading."

Rob's statements echoed those I hear every week from many of my clients, with diverse occupations and lifestyles. When I went home that afternoon, I found myself researching recent studies on stress. I found that what Rob and so many of my clients are expressing is not only typical, it is now an epidemic. This book began on that one long bicycle ride up a difficult hill.

WHAT'S GOING ON?

The amount of stress experienced by people in America and throughout the world is rapidly rising. We work too much, sleep too little, love with half a heart, and wonder why we are unhappy and unhealthy.

Half of Americans indicate they lie awake at night because of stress, and three-quarters experience stress symptoms — physical, psychological, or both. A survey on stress conducted by Harris Interactive for the American Psychological Association in 2012 indicates high stress levels among Americans, with 53 percent saying they have little or no support for stress management from their health care provider.[1] Roughly 70 percent of Americans hate their jobs and feel disengaged, according to a 2013 Gallup poll, and two-thirds of office visits to primary care doctors are stress-related.[2] According to the World Health Organization, Americans die sooner and have higher rates of disease than residents of sixteen other affluent countries.

Stress in and of itself is not the issue; the problem lies in how we perceive and react to stress and its potential consequences. Researchers at the University of Wisconsin conducted studies that indicate that stress increases the risk of dying by 43 percent, but only for those who believed that stress was harmful.[3]

We know that personal and professional success does not come without sacrifice and stress, but it should not ruin our health and leave our relationships devoid of love and intimacy. We need to go beyond the pursuit of material rewards to achieving genuine, healthy successes throughout all aspects of life. Many people throughout the world are discovering that what they thought would bring them happiness has trapped them in an emotional, stress-filled prison. Fortunately, there is still a path forward.

HOW DO WE CHANGE?
INTRODUCING THE CONCEPT OF EMPATHIC CBT

In this book I present an approach to reducing stress that I call *empathic cognitive behavioral therapy* (CBT). Empathic CBT will help you take steps to free yourself from the stress caused by the obsession to excel and begin the process of finding meaning in your work and in your relationships. This new combination of the power of empathy and cognitive behavioral therapy will provide you with a comprehensive self-help tool to reduce stress and balance your life. Empathy calms the emotional brain so that we can perceive situations and interactions accurately and thoughtfully. With empathy, we produce our own natural stress-reducing chemicals that create calm, focused energy, allowing us to do and be our best. When we have developed our understanding and practice of empathy, we can employ CBT to correct distorted thinking. These two processes create a synergy that reduces the stress in our lives and helps us realize our potential.

I have been working with clients using empathic CBT for more than thirty-five years. If you commit to doing the necessary work, this unique approach will enable you to lessen the stress in your relationships, family, and work life.

EMPATHY

Empathy is the capacity to understand and respond to the unique experiences of another person. It is the force that motivates us to perform acts of compassion and altruism. Empathy is part of our genetic endowment: it is not an emotion or a feeling but a capacity that is innately present.

Empathy is frequently confused with sympathy, but the two are different. Sympathy is the capacity to identify with another person's experience even when we do not actually know whether our experiences are similar. For example, sympathy is at work if you hear of a neighbor's father passing away and immediately respond, "She must be devastated! I certainly was when my father died." A few days later, though, you might hear that your neighbor's father left the family when she was a baby and seldom had any contact with his daughter. In fact, and I emphasize the word *fact*, she was not devastated at all by his death. Where sympathy rushes in, empathy takes time to understand the facts. Sympathy, which is often driven by immediate emotion without considering the facts of a situation, can cause more harm than good. Generalizations are the last thing people want to hear when they long to be understood.

Empathy is objective. It is not based on assumptions but on truth. Empathy slows down emotion to a manageable degree so that thought and cognition can perceive accurately. Empathy is centered on the uniqueness of the other person's experience: it is a thoughtful response rather than a quick general reaction. "I know what you're going through" is a familiar sympathetic comment that people often express when they identify with a situation.

We are born with the capacity for empathy. If that capacity is not developed, however, it will atrophy like an unused muscle. I know, from leading group therapy sessions for more than twenty-five years, that human beings can be taught how to expand their empathic range in ways that reap profound benefits. Empathy plays a crucial role in the reduction of stress from the moment of birth. Babies cannot lessen their stress by themselves: they need the empathy of caregivers to calm and soothe them. Early in life, children learn that empathic connections ease pain and lessen stress. When empathy is absent in early years, children are at risk for an assortment of illnesses.

We also know that stress, both acute and chronic, impairs empathic accuracy. Worry about stressors draws a person's cognitive effort away from deciphering other people's behavioral cues in everyday interactions. In essence, when we are stressed, we lose our ability to perceive emotional cues: our attention is compromised, and we are unable to comprehend situations and interactions as we might when we are calm.

> Empathy plays a crucial role in the reduction of stress from the moment of birth. Babies cannot lessen their stress by themselves: they need the empathy of caregivers to calm and soothe them.

We know that empathy is the brain's salve for limiting aggression; its inhibitory effect produces successful negotiation rather than needless confrontation. This effect is especially valuable in the business world, where teamwork and collaboration are of great importance. We know that so-called empathy organizations like IBM and Harley-Davidson create a work culture in which employees are quick to grasp opportunities, react to change with less anxiety, and feel a sense of purpose that fuels a positive work environment.

Empathy must be put into action: being empathic is more important than having empathy and remaining passive. Because empathy is truth-oriented and gives us the opportunity to perceive clearly and objectively, it is the ideal complement to cognitive behavior therapy.

When we give and receive empathy, transformation occurs. An empathic interaction produces calming brain chemicals that create a sense of security and positive feelings. These brain changes make us happier and more resilient. As you will see in chapter 12, giving in an empathic way lessens stress. But it is equally important to our health to have people in our lives who behave empathically toward us.

We learn to become more empathic when we slow down, become present, and are fully committed to understanding another person's uniqueness. Only through practicing empathic listening (see chapter 3) can we move beyond the surface and into another human being's heart.

The deep emotional learning that conditions us to hold on to past hurts — the brain's negativity bias — can be released and understood permanently only with the understanding that empathy provides. We can correct distorted thinking with CBT techniques, but the emotional part of the brain will return to negativity if the situations that hurt us deeply are not understood and resolved on both the emotional and cognitive levels. Understanding needs to precede explaining. The heart of empathy is understanding, created by a sense of rapport with others. They can provide objective feedback to help us gain insight into the reasons why some emotional hurts are so hard to heal.

Once understanding is established, including awareness of how past hurts influence our perceptions of the present, CBT can provide insights into the accuracy of our views of both ourselves and others. Retraining both your heart and your head is incredibly powerful and will alter your life in very positive ways. Several studies have indicated that CBT is effective in the short run, but that psychodynamic therapies — those that acknowledge and examine the effect of the past on the present — are more effective in the long term. Combining the use of empathy with CBT ensures the best outcome in the shortest time.

CBT

CBT is different from traditional talk therapy in that it deemphasizes exploration of the past and focuses on the way a person thinks. The principle behind CBT is that thoughts influence feelings, and feelings influence our actions and our interpretations of situations. It is not situations or interactions with people that determine how we feel and lead our lives: it's how we perceive, interpret, and think about our experiences. CBT emphasizes the influence of our thoughts on our behavior and holds that when dysfunctional thinking is corrected, behavior and mood improve. Clients are also engaged in a more active way than in traditional therapy. CBT focuses on developing strategies to cope with specific problems. It typically involves homework assignments to practice new skills and to reinforce the view that change is an active process. Therapy is seen as a cooperative effort in which the client and therapist agree on which issues are most important to address and set specific goals. Unlike traditional therapy, however, CBT can be practiced without a therapist through instructional books, computer programs, and workshops.

CBT has been documented as effective in addressing depression, anxiety, eating disorders, low back pain, substance abuse, fibromyalgia, and some personality disorders, in addition to being helpful in treating psychotic conditions. There has been less evidence-based research on the effectiveness of CBT in treating stress. Interestingly, the Beck Institute, founded to advance the practice of CBT, lists seventy-six adult, child, and adolescent disorders that CBT can treat successfully, but stress is not included. Clearly, with the statistics I have listed above, we need an effective CBT model to address the growing epidemic of stress throughout the world.

One of the criticisms of CBT, despite its overall success, is that the changes created may not endure because the therapy fails to address emotionally conditioned learning, which is quite difficult to overwrite. Empathic CBT addresses this issue comprehensively so that the emotional, conditioned negative learning highlighted by Aaron Beck (one of the originators of cognitive behavior therapy) and others can be understood and changed in a lasting fashion.

Empathic CBT is, in essence, the best of both worlds: without belaboring the past as in psychoanalysis, it acknowledges the effects of that past so that their interference with the accurate perception of ourselves and others can be corrected.

In the chapters that follow, I integrate the dynamics of empathy and CBT and explain the positive changes that this approach produces in our brains. I share the stories of several of my clients who have found the way back to a wholesome, satisfying life, free of excessive stress. The stories of these courageous individuals will show you how you can change your life from one filled with tension to one characterized by peace of mind and minimal stress.

> Empathic CBT is, in essence, the best of both worlds: without belaboring the past as in psychoanalysis, it acknowledges the effects of that past so that their interference with the accurate perception of ourselves and others can be corrected.

ENGAGING THE THINKING AND EMOTIONAL BRAINS

Empathic CBT first addresses past hurts that interfere with accurate views of yourself and others. Once these hurts are resolved, you can begin to correct the distortions in thinking they have created. Standard CBT begins without the strong foundation created by resolving past hurts. Empathic CBT not only addresses the interference of past hurts, but it also allows you to be free to change the original story you wrote about yourself, with the biases that past hurts create. In the process you also change your brain chemistry, reduce stress hormones, and create more soothing brain chemicals that foster positive thinking and overall well-being.

Do you remember every time you have been hurt deeply in your life? I am guessing your answer is yes. Do you remember each time you have been given a compliment? I am guessing you do not. Your hurts are stored in the emotional center of the brain so that you will be protected against similar hurts in the future. The problem is that this collection of painful memories leads to theories about human nature — what Aaron Beck calls a *negative schema*. Hurts experienced in childhood or adolescence lead to the formation of a negative view of life, and this negative view is reactivated when you are stressed in adult life. A negative schema creates *cognitive bias*, which is a dysfunctional thinking pattern that can cause stress, anxiety, and depression. You may live your whole life believing in the distorted, fictional story you wrote about yourself at a time when you could not possibly see yourself and your potential accurately.

> Your hurts are stored in the emotional center of the brain so that you will be protected against similar hurts in the future.

This negative schema creates stress, which has a neurochemical impact because it causes the release of the stress hormone cortisol. High levels of cortisol kill neurons in the memory center of the brain; the unfortunate result is that your ability to think clearly or creatively is compromised. Cortisol causes fewer synapses (structures that pass messages from one neuron to another) to be developed. As your brain uses and reinforces the same neural pathways, it is difficult for you to think of new solutions to your problems, which makes you more prone to negative thinking and to developing a perpetual stress response. This schema can in turn cause communication breakdowns. Cortisol also binds negative memories, making for a stubborn, entrenched negative view of yourself.

Part of the power of negative thinking derives from the evolution of our brain. Because the brain is programmed to protect us from further hurts, it is wired biologically to record negative experiences with greater intensity. This tendency may also lead to mistaken perceptions that arise because of assumptions about what we expect to happen, as opposed to what actually does happen. Past disappointments or emotional pain can program our brains to jump to conclusions when we sense similar circumstances in the present. This tendency has been referred to as the brain's negative feedback loop. Stress also affects the hippocampus, the memory center of the brain. This part of the brain is also bathed in stress hormones, causing stress to be associated with particular situations.

Research indicates that CBT can positively affect this part of the brain and the prefrontal cortex, which helps in managing self-control, but several studies indicate that traditional psychodynamic psychotherapy yields better results in the long term. Traditional therapy is oriented toward gaining insight and awareness from uncovering emotional hurts from the past that influence our feelings and behavior in the present. For instance, a woman who grew up with an alcoholic father and then married an alcoholic husband may realize through therapy that she has been conditioned to rescue men who have alcohol problems. A combination of several reports comparing CBT and traditional psychotherapy for depression found that people who used the traditional approach experienced larger improvements in the long term. The difference may be that emotional hurts are more likely to be explored in depth with psychodynamic psychotherapy, with a particular emphasis on gaining insight and improving awareness of causes of distress.

Psychodynamic approaches accent cause and effect, exploring the ways in which the past influences the present, whereas CBT focuses almost exclusively on changing dysfunctional thinking and actions that influence a person's mood and behavior in the present. Another study of marriage therapy found that 38 percent of couples using CBT-type behavioral strategies were divorced four years later, compared to just 3 percent of couples who relied on insight-oriented traditional therapy.[4]

Empathic CBT eliminates the concerns of these studies, as it engages the amygdala — the emotional part of the brain and the center for conditioned dysfunctional learning. Emotional conditioned learning is learning accompanied by intense emotion. This releases the stress hormone cortisol, which encodes memory deep in the memory center of the brain.

Empathic CBT will teach you how to change your neurochemistry naturally — how to produce the hormones that provide a calm, focused state of mind, rather than a state that causes distress and discomfort. Empathic CBT will take you on a journey that has the potential to affect both the thinking and the emotional brain, reversing false beliefs and freeing your mind of distorted views that have compromised your life.

GETTING THE MOST OUT OF THIS BOOK

In the following chapters I offer background research, examples, and analysis to help you understand the causes and sources of stress and how to address it. But the real secret to understanding yourself and bringing about change through empathic CBT lies in putting these ideas into action. At the end of each chapter, I ask you to complete some cognitive behavioral exercises. These can help you reduce your stress without ever stepping into a psychologist's office.

The exercises ask you to examine past and recent events and record your thoughts and actions. They ask you to identify habitual cognitive distortions (biases in the way you think) that you use. For instance, did you personalize a situation, use mind reading, label your behavior or other people's negatively, or use black-and-white thinking? (See the Cognitive Distortions Glossary on page xxiii.)

Emotional conditioned learning is learning accompanied by intense emotion. This releases the stress hormone cortisol, which encodes memory deep in the memory center of the brain.

When you finish the book I ask you to complete two additional exercises: the False Core Belief Exercise and the Reinforcing New Beliefs Exercise starting on page 181 in the Appendix.

The exercises also present questions for you to explore in a personal journal. If you don't already keep a journal, now is a good time to start. Putting pen to paper has proved to be healing by helping to release emotion and gain insight. Several studies in recent years have indicated that journal writing improves immune function and increases levels of alertness, determination, and energy while providing emotional release. Please try to answer all the journal questions at the end of each chapter, and remember that you will gain far more if you share your answers with someone close to you.

The final exercise is a "take action" step to put into practice what you have learned. A peaceful state of mind is achieved not only through changing negative thinking but also through positive actions. New research indicates that building optimism and resilience requires not just thought but also action.

Cognitive Distortions Glossary

This glossary defines terms used throughout the book. You may want to refer back to it as you read.

assumed similarity: Thinking that other people believe and perceive the same way you do

black-and-white thinking: Categorizing outcomes with the assumptions that things will be either good or bad

catastrophizing: Magnifying problems and assuming everything will end in a very negative way

cognitive conformity: Seeing the world the way you believe that those around you see it

emotional reasoning: Basing conclusions about yourself and other people on your feelings, without thoughtfully examining the objective accuracy of your perceptions

fortune telling: Making predictions about the future, usually negative ones

idealization: Overvaluing other people and diminishing yourself

ignoring situational or contextual factors: Believing that circumstances and outcomes are due solely to your behavior or competence level

ignoring the positive: Dismissing any positive information and always looking at the negative side of situations

in-group bias: Trusting and believing in people who are in your circle, without objective assessment of beliefs and opinions

labeling: Labeling your behavior and the behavior of others in a negative way

magnifying: Viewing your mistakes as greater than they are in reality

microsecond reactions: Quick reactions that are ruled by emotions with little thought involved, often governed by old conditioning

mind reading: Assuming you know what other people are thinking

minimizing: Making less of anything you accomplish

negatively biased recall: humans' hardwired tendency to record and recall negative events more quickly and deeply than positive ones

negative predictions: Overestimating the chances that a behavior or action will have a negative outcome

overgeneralization: Assuming that what has occurred once will always occur and that something that has never taken place will never happen

oversimplification: Describing a person, problem, or situation in a way that leaves out vital facts, making it seem far less complicated than it actually is

overthinking: Believing that your obsessive thinking will lead to positive outcomes

performance addiction: The irrational belief, learned early in life and reinforced by cultural expectations, that perfecting your appearance and achieving status will secure love and respect from others

personalization and blame: Believing that situations are out of your control or blaming others for events you think are in their control

projection: Defending against unpleasant impulses or feelings by denying their occurrence and/or attributing them to others

self-criticism as motivation: Believing that self-criticism is a positive motivator resulting in positive outcomes

shoulds and musts: Holding strong beliefs about how you and others should behave; thinking in absolutes

CHAPTER 1

Why *You* Should Care about Stress

> You cannot heal what you do not acknowledge, and what you do not consciously acknowledge will remain in control of you from within, festering and destroying you and those around you.
>
> RICHARD ROHR, *Breathing under Water*

We often use the word *stress* casually, with little acknowledgment of its adverse effects. We even describe our stress in dismissive ways. For instance, a Fortune 500 executive may walk in the door after work looking distraught, and when her husband asks what is wrong, she may say, "Oh, I'm just stressed out with stuff at the office." An accountant may tells his client, "Don't worry; everyone's a little stressed during tax season." A single mom may sit by the side of the pool flipping through a magazine with an ad for an upcoming cruise that says, "Escape from the stresses of life." If only it were that simple.

It's not that we don't acknowledge the prevalence of stress: we've been doing so for decades. The cover story of *Time* magazine for the week of June 6, 1983, proclaimed that stress was the "epidemic of the Eighties," as Americans were "seeking cures for modern anxieties." More than thirty years later, stress is still wreaking havoc. All demographics — adolescents, young professionals, middle-aged workers, and retirees — are at risk from this silent and cumulative killer.

In 1994, the *Harvard Business Review* cited evidence that 60 to 90 percent of doctors' visits were tied to the effects of stress. Today, 66 percent of visits to primary care doctors are stress-related, and 50 percent of American workers say they stay awake at night troubled by physical or emotional effects of stress.[1]

The physical repercussions of stress are indeed startling. These include:

- a decrease in immune system functionality
- heightened risk of heart disease and diabetes
- a spike in stress hormones that increase the risk of cancer

The potential to lose years of your life due to stress is very real.

In addition, occupational stress subjects you to cognitive symptoms of stress, including the following:

- repeated worrying
- weakened performance
- lack of judgment
- memory problems

Stress also plagues families and relationships by aggravating emotional symptoms such as excessive moodiness, irritability, and interpersonal conflict. These effects of stress influence how we relate to and how we are received by those close to us.

Deep down, you know that stress — perhaps even in a chronic form — has been crippling you. You know it because you feel it, and you are not alone. Two-thirds of adult Americans experiencing elevated stress levels report that their stress has escalated in the past year, according to a recent survey by the American Psychological Association.[2]

But unless you are among the only 17 percent of Americans who actually talk to their health care providers about stress, it's likely that you try to ignore the problems that stress has the potential to unleash.

The most common areas of stress, according to the American Psychological Association's yearly studies, are money, family, and relationships. In essence, if you struggle financially or have family and relationship difficulties, then you are among the many who are not mentally ill but are instead suffering from chronic stress.[3]

Psychologists have identified key variables that determine whether stress ultimately affects us positively or negatively:

- our perception of stress
- the meaning we attach to it
- our ability to cope with uncertainty and ambiguity
- the degree of control we have over the circumstances that produce stress

RONDA, A TYPICAL EXAMPLE

Ronda, a thirty-six-year-old mother of three, manages her art studio most weekdays and tries to get to the gym a few times a week, but she has been unable to do so with consistency. She worries about her overworked and highly stressed husband, Steve, who has not exercised in the last few years even though he knows the risks posed by his high blood pressure and high cholesterol levels. He is a committed father, but as a software sales representative for a large corporation, he travels frequently and is not available to help with the children as much as they both would like.

Ronda worries about her mother, who is in an unstable second marriage, and about her biological father, who remains unemployed and gets by doing odd jobs. She recently discovered that her father has occasionally been borrowing money from her husband. Steve's dad died two years ago, and Steve, as an only son, also feels responsible for taking care of his mother's needs and her home.

Ronda is very attractive, engaging, college-educated, and a former soccer player; you would assume on meeting her that she's in great health and quite happy. And the truth is that when she can calm down and catch her breath, she truly is quite happy, and she loves her husband and children. Most of her days, however, are spent rushing around, trying to make appointments on time and fulfill the many responsibilities of her daily life. Studies have shown that women tend to have higher rates of stress than men, with the key worries being money and paying bills.

Steve is an affable person, easy to like, but his self-care habits have deteriorated significantly, so that he now experiences back pain and difficulty relaxing. He often says kiddingly, "Stress is my middle name."

Ronda has recently begun suffering from tension headaches. Her memory has also failed her, which greatly increases her anxiety and lessens her confidence in her abilities: "I hope I'm not going senile, honestly — I have forgotten two appointments for the children in the last week, and my own dentist's appointment, and I am so spacey, it is scaring me."

THE COSTS OF STRESS

The story of Ronda and Steve is typical of many young couples today. They are not mentally ill, and they do not need psychiatric medication, but they are aware of problems with their bodies and minds and are at a loss to explain or remedy them.

Regardless of age, our fast-paced lifestyle emphasizes achievement at all costs. We have high expectations of ourselves, driven by media and social-media images of the perfect life. In addition, many Americans are isolated: most people now have fewer close friends than in previous years. These pressures affect our sense of self, increasing the degree of stress we feel. No one is immune. The effects of stress can be devastating to our entire being, regardless of age, gender, or occupation.

Knowing how stress affects the brain and body will help you understand how you can limit the stress response. Stress begins in the amygdala, the emotional center of the brain. If your amygdala perceives a threat, whether it is the sound of footsteps behind you on a deserted street at night or a friend making a humiliating comment about you in the presence of others, it springs into action immediately. The amygdala sends a signal to the hypothalamus, a section of the brain that regulates hormone output. The hypothalamus alerts the adrenal glands to release the stress hormones cortisol and adrenaline. These stress hormones are released whether the threat is real or imagined. Training ourselves to distinguish between real and imaginary threats is a vital skill, and one that the use of empathy and CBT can help us develop.

Adrenaline raises your heart rate and blood pressure, and cortisol sends a surge of sugar to the blood to cope with physical demands. As this almost instantaneous reaction takes place, your immune system, digestion, sex drive, and other functions are put on hold. Memory, learning, and, most important, the ability to be empathic are compromised.

A survey conducted by researchers at Stanford University revealed disturbing results among ten- to fourteen-year-old girls, comparing those from households with stressed mothers to those raised in homes with little maternal stress. The participants from stressed homes showed premature cellular aging, equivalent to about six years of biological age.[4] Stress also affects the immune system, leading to inflammation that can increase the proliferation of cancer cells. In one study of stress, one group of mice was subjected to stress by being isolated from others. All the mice were then injected with cells from human tumors. The researchers found that tumors were more likely

> Stress hormones are released whether the threat is real or imagined.

to grow in the stressed mice. Among pregnant mice, those with increased stress hormones showed a decrease in fetal weight.[5]

Research further indicates that stress can cause:

- heart disease
- weight gain
- diabetes
- dementia
- anxiety
- depression
- hair loss

In addition, a 2015 study conducted by the Harvard and Stanford business schools examined job stresses and the relationship of the mental and physical effects of stress to mortality. The researchers found that the physical problems caused by work stress led to fatal conditions that accounted for 120,000 deaths each year, making work-related stress more deadly than Alzheimer's, influenza, or diabetes. Stress-related health issues are estimated to incur $180 billion of health care costs each year.[6]

Finally, researchers are starting to find that long-term stress can have serious effects on the brain. The brain and the immune system are connected. Cells called microglia, which were thought to merely protect the immune system, are now known to make up 15 percent of our brain cells. Microglia cells help the brain repair damaged neurons, but if they are activated too often by stress, they produce inflammation in the brain. Researchers at Ruhr University Bochum have linked inflamed microglia cells to Alzheimer's disease, multiple sclerosis, and schizophrenia.[7]

Good people like Ronda and Steve, and millions of others throughout the world, are suffering from a devastating condition that we must and can change. Yet 79 percent of Americans try to deal with stress on their own, never asking for or knowing how to obtain help. It is time for us to get serious about reducing stress, using the techniques of empathic CBT.

As you read through this book, remember that to rid yourself of undue stress, you need to do the exercises in each chapter. Not only will these exercises reinforce the concepts presented and help you gain perspective on the specific sources and effects of your own stress, but they will also help you gain a greater sense of control over your life. A study by Steve Maier of the University of Colorado indicates that the degree of control we feel over stress determines the degree to which we are affected physiologically. His research, and that of many other scientists, indicates that uncontrollable stressors are destructive, whereas stress that feels escapable is less damaging.[8] Perception of control is the key to managing stress and being able to tolerate the uncertainty that is part of life.

Perception of control is the key to managing stress and being able to tolerate the uncertainty that is part of life.

It will take time to gain control and change the way you perceive stress. Please do not rush through this book as if it were a competition. Settle in, calm yourself, and complete a chapter every few days. If you rush, you will only continue the cycle of stress. Let us get started with balance and calm energy.

To begin with, please take the Stress Questionnaire in the appendix (page 176) to establish a baseline measure of your current stress levels. Then, as you work through the book, you can repeat the questionnaire and monitor your progress.

CHAPTER 2

Expanding Our Humanity
The Discipline of Empathy

> When you show deep empathy toward others, their defensive energy
> goes down, and positive energy replaces it. That's when you can get
> more creative in solving problems.
>
> STEPHEN COVEY, *The 7 Habits of Highly Effective People*

Empathy guides us in the accurate understanding of situations and
relationships. When we live with empathy, we realize that it is a
kind of virtual reality: we put ourselves in the other person's shoes,
absorbing her experience, observing the world through her eyes,
feeling her emotions, and imagining thinking her thoughts.

Empathy is also the key to negotiating and resolving conflict,
whether between couples, communities, states, or countries — expanding our capacity to understand the person or groups we encounter.

Empathy is not, however, a tool or a technique that can be easily
mastered. Empathy is instead an innate capacity that requires careful nurturing and constant attention. Empathy is a way of keeping
our balance, which in turn helps others become balanced when they
have lost their way.

Several studies have demonstrated that when you believe that
empathy can be learned and that your capacity for empathy can
grow, you are far more likely to expand your empathic range.

Empathy training teaches you to limit the influence of the primitive brain, using the neocortex — the thinking brain — to perceive reality accurately, without emotion or distortion. In a study in monkeys in which the neural wiring that supports empathy was severed, the monkeys could not interpret other animals' friendly or hostile behavior. They lived in isolation, ruled by the primitive brain's emotions of anger and fear.[1]

> Empathy training teaches you to limit the influence of the primitive brain, using the neocortex – the thinking brain – to perceive reality accurately, without emotion or distortion.

As our lives become more hectic, we sleep less and eat haphazardly, and our mood suffers. When we are angry or detached, our empathy suffers too. We must learn to slow down so that we can think clearly and react appropriately to a given situation. Most often we need the help of others to slow down and calm ourselves, confiding in those close to us so that we can begin the process of dissipating stress.

For Ronda and Steve, empathy suffers because of Steve's business travel. When they part on Sunday night, the family exchanges big hugs and loving kisses. Then Steve heads off to the airport, returning late on Thursday night. Ronda often feels increasingly frustrated as the week goes by. Steve, meanwhile, gets tired of sleeping in hotels and being away from his family, and he often feels he can't tolerate one more dinner listening to his customer telling the same stories. Both Ronda and Steve experience increasing stress levels that affect their communications. As the days pass, the text messages, phone calls, and evening Skype sessions have less warmth than earlier in the week.

When Steve arrives home at 11:30 PM on Thursday night, he is exhausted, and so is Ronda. She tries to stay awake to greet him, but she is dying to go to bed. Instead of greeting him with empathy, she keeps preparing the kids' lunches without looking up. Feeling offended, he withdraws into his cave space in his finished basement.

Ronda finishes her chores and mumbles good night to him

downstairs; he says the same. He sits up watching sports highlights on ESPN until 1:00 AM and falls asleep on the couch, while she sleeps alone in their bedroom. They both awaken during the night with a sense of exasperation. In the morning, they interact with the kids but are somewhat terse with each other. He hugs her good-bye, and she softens as she feels his touch. He heads off to work with an ache in his heart, not knowing that she is feeling the same way.

Empathy, and the understanding and positive neurochemicals it produces, cannot exist in the absence of trust and a sense of security, and these diminish when a person feels slighted or hurt. When we can empathize, we are less likely to be offended. We look beyond the surface to see what is affecting the other person. If, however, we are depleted and stressed, as Steve and Ronda both are, our empathic range becomes narrower. What we hear and perceive is greatly influenced by our emotions and by stress hormones.

SECONDHAND STRESS: THE RIPPLE EFFECT

Secondhand stress is becoming common in our tension-filled society. Our nervous systems talk to each other, and the stress of one person can easily affect others. Parents pass their stress to their children, spouses to each other, colleagues to colleagues, friends to friends. Increases in inflammation and blood pressure have been noted in couples who stress each other. Researchers at the University of Michigan noted that 33 percent of husbands and 26 percent of wives had high blood pressure in 2006, whereas in 2010 rates rose to 37 percent for men and 30 percent for women.[2] Steve and Ronda are excellent examples of how stress passes between partners and then to the worlds they move in. Steve carries his low mood into his office, and Ronda carries hers to work. The children feel the tension between their parents as they get on the school bus. This state of mind will likely affect the children's ability to learn and their parents' performance at work.

In order to regulate our neurochemistry so that we can feel calm, energetic, and creative, we need to balance our brain chemistry to protect ourselves and to be resilient when exposed to other people's stress. This is not to say that we should be indifferent to others. Rather I am emphasizing that our state of mind, whenever we encounter the emotions of others, has a great impact on our health and on our ability to react positively to others in difficult times. Sleep, exercise, proper nutrition, meaningful work, and positive relationships are all critical factors in determining the range of our empathy as we go through the day.

EMPATHY TO THE RESCUE

Awareness of our state of mind is critical to managing our reactions and our ability to be empathic. For instance, Ronda knew she was exhausted before Steve got home. What if she had sent a text, or, even better, called Steve and said, "Honey, I'm sure you're exhausted. I am, too. Do you mind if I go to bed, and we can catch up in the morning?" Steve might have been disappointed, but since he too was exhausted, he might have felt relieved to be able to just come home and go to bed himself. If they had waited to catch up until the morning, when they were refreshed, the whole day could have been different.

When we are depleted, we cannot see beyond the surface of another person's experience. However, if we teach ourselves to recognize our mental state, we can slow down, become introspective, and see beyond our self-absorption.

To encourage awareness of how mental and bodily depletion can affect our mood and vulnerability, Alcoholics Anonymous (AA) uses the mnemonic *HALT*. These four letters stand for "hungry, angry, lonely, and tired." The lesson is to not take any action when you find yourself in any of these states of mind. Instead, AA recommends that you back up and collect yourself, increasing your awareness of how compromised you are and whether you are likely to say or do something you will regret.

TAMING A BAD MOOD AND UNDERSTANDING UNRESOLVED HURTS

In order to cope effectively with another person's negative mood, you need to be careful not to respond with anger when another person directs anger toward you but instead to try to understand and respond to the underlying issues producing the other person's anger. When you recognize that anger often covers hurt, disappointment, and insecurity, you can address those feelings instead of reacting with equal anger.

This ability begins at home. If Ronda and Steve communicate with empathy, their children will gain a priceless understanding of human nature. If Steve, noticing that Ronda is responding with an edge in her voice, could ask Ronda what is bothering or hurting her rather than responding in kind, he might prevent an argument and instead stimulate a productive conversation. People often appreciate the efforts we make to help rather than respond in ways that worsen an already tense situation. Empathy allows us to see beyond the surface while allowing those we love to make mistakes without worrying about retaliation.

Empathy allows us to see beyond the surface while allowing those we love to make mistakes without worrying about retaliation.

ANGER, HURT, AND EMPATHY

Anger can block the flow of empathy. Extensive research has revealed that when people are angry, their attempts to resolve conflict are accompanied by quick judgments and oversimplifications. Anger also has harmful effects on the immune and cardiovascular system and long-term effects on brain chemistry. Research by the cardiologist Redford Williams of Duke University Medical Center showed that the stress hormone adrenaline, when released in anger, causes stored memories to become more vivid and harder to erase than less emotional memories.[3]

Take my client Mary, for example. She describes herself as having been a kind, fun-loving young child, known for nurturing her sister and having a strong attachment to both parents. Then, in her late childhood, Mary's parents divorced. Her father seldom saw his children and frequently broke his promises to visit them. As a result, Mary grew up with a distrust of men, which frequently resulted in tantrums when she was slighted by boyfriends. Her negative view of life dominated her adult years, and today her natural good nature has all but disappeared. Going from breakup to breakup, Mary is disheartened and repeatedly confirmed in her view that men are basically bad.

When hurts accumulate without a positive resolution, we often lose ourselves in self-absorption and resentment. This kind of preoccupation is a tremendous drain on mental energy, leaving us with little capacity for interest in others. Anger can turn to tolerance, however, when our perceptions change from fear to truth. When we stop seeing others through the hurts of the past, when generalizations cease and we begin to perceive more objectively, we become more hopeful and optimistic. We feel closer to the people in our lives as we recover trust. Trust is often correlated with happiness in communities and individuals. When we trust others, we feel safe and calm. We can then perceive more accurately and thoughtfully. What we feel inside determines what we see outside.

Once a person like Mary harbors unresolved hurts, her anger and sense of helplessness can dramatically change the way she thinks and behaves. The psychologist Paul Levine and his colleagues at the Foundation of Human Enrichment have demonstrated that a fixation on major or minor hurts makes people shun intimacy and aggravates stress. Dr. Levine's work demonstrates how even a trauma victim can return to a state of calm through meaningful contact with an empathic, understanding individual. Such relationships make us more reflective and enable us to embark on a journey to learn what has troubled us, how to resolve our hurts, and how to move on.

Sadness is often seen as synonymous with depression. Depression is often, in fact, an attempt to avoid sadness. Sadness is the body's cue to stop, think, and work through what is troubling us. People who don't heed this cue avoid examining their troubles, and the stress caused by avoidance becomes a way of life. In essence, depression is often avoidance of using the information that sadness can provide.

Mary's sadness arises from the fact that she never dealt with the divorce of her parents. Understandably, she ran away from her own sadness, but she has paid a high price ever since. She has become self-absorbed and stunted with anger. She has lost her ability to do good for others and can no longer see the goodness in others or herself.

We cannot resolve our hurts alone. Without input from others, we repeat our thought patterns over and over again and remain stuck in the mud of our own negativity. This is a formula for continual stress. By releasing ourselves from the mistaken beliefs that support our uneasiness with people, however, we reawaken our basic goodness and allow love and compassion to break through. Our empathic breakthrough then removes the obstacles to seeing our world and ourselves clearly. If Mary had allowed herself to be open and vulnerable, to share her hurts with others and accept empathic feedback — a courageous step, for sure — she might have

We cannot resolve our hurts alone. Without input from others, we repeat our thought patterns over and over again and remain stuck in the mud of our own negativity. This is a formula for continual stress.

been able to recover the spirit for living she once possessed. Her story is an example of how holding on to anger and resentment ties us to the past and the story we created when emotionally distraught.

Before moving on to the next chapter, please take the Empathy Quotient Questionnaire in the appendix (page 173) and record your answers. Retake the questionnaire after completing the book, and compare your scores. Research from the Harvard Business School has found that EQ counts twice as much as IQ in predicting success in the work world.[4]

CHAPTER 3

Empathic Listening
Loving Away Stress

Holy Listening — to listen another's soul into life, into a condition
of disclosure and discovery, may be almost the greatest service that
any human being ever performs for another.

DOUGLAS STEERE, *On Listening to Another*

I am going to tell a story about my mother. I hope it conveys the
value of knowing how to listen, how empathic listening creates a
sense of calm in both parties, and how giving in this way creates
lasting connections that make us more resilient and less likely to be
hampered in our lives by stress.

LEARNING FROM AN EMPATHIC MOTHER

My career path began in my home, observing how my parents inter-
acted with family, friends, and strangers. As a young man, I began
to study psychology, and as I entered graduate school, my maternal
grandfather died of liver cancer. When I returned to my parents'
home for the funeral services, my mother called me aside and made
a provocative statement.

She said, "You are studying human nature; if you keep your
eyes and heart open during the next few days, you may learn more

17

about people than you ever will in a classroom." She mentioned my grandfather's wealth and his numerous business friends, and she reminded me that my grandmother had a fatal heart attack several years previously. Shortly before her death, she had found a letter from her husband's mistress in his suit jacket. My mother always said she died of a broken heart. This conclusion seemed strange to me at the time, but in retrospect, I believe it was the case. (Scientists have since identified the condition *broken heart syndrome*, or stress cardiomyopathy, which can be fatal. The left ventricle takes on an unusual shape because of an excess of stress hormones in the system. Ninety percent of cases occur in postmenopausal women, like my fifty-two-year-old grandmother.)[1]

On the day of my grandfather's funeral, my mother asked me if I was impressed with his life. I knew enough to delay answering that question. I just waited for her to deliver what I expected would be a valuable piece of wisdom. "Pay attention," she said, "to how many people shed tears throughout the next three days, and we will talk later about what kind of person your grandfather was." I did, and after two days of an afternoon and evening wake, and one day of a funeral with many people attending, I did not see one tear being shed.

I knew that my grandfather had been known as a highly stressed, shrewd businessperson who had extramarital affairs and took little interest in his children or grandchildren. I remember him once dropping in unexpectedly and my mother cooking for him while he talked and she listened. If she tried to talk, he interrupted and continued telling one of his familiar stories about someone who had caused him grief in his business dealings. In essence, she was the audience for his accounts of his stressful life.

My mother left school in the seventh grade to go to work. She never saw the inside of a high school classroom, but the wisdom she imparted set the stage for a young man to realize that true success in life is a complicated endeavor. My mother died at fifty-nine, after breast cancer had spread to her bones. In the last days of her life, her oncologist, who had become very attached to her, told me that she just could not tell my mother alone that her cancer had metastasized. She asked if I would be with her to deliver the news. My mother's first response was, "What about Erica?" She couldn't believe that she would miss all the joy of watching our three-year-old grow up. Her immediate reaction to knowing she was dying was sadness at not being able to love her granddaughter as she grew up. As my mother was crying, I could hear Erica's footsteps in the hallway as the nurses chased her. Looking into the unbearable pain in my mother's eyes and hearing the laughter of our child, filling the hall with joy as only a young child's giggle can, was a moment of emotional paralysis. That moment is forever etched in my mind as proof that empathy — the ability to listen and enter another's world — is intimately linked to joy.

My mother lived a life of giving. She didn't know how to be any other way. In the end, she not only developed a relationship with her Egyptian oncologist but was also clearly a favorite of all the nurses and doctors who treated her. She kept listening and giving, even in her final hours, and she kept receiving. At her wake, my father turned to me, pointing to the long line of people approaching her casket, and muttered, "This is like being at the League of Nations." He noted that there were people of all races and divergent backgrounds and religions, and she had befriended them all. At her funeral, our local priest stated that he could sum up the whole of her life in two words: "Simply profound." And, unlike the death of her materially successful father, her passing caused oceans of tears.

On the afternoon of my mother's wake, a young surgeon told me that my mother had changed his life. She worked in an emergency room of a small community hospital, taking information for incoming patients. In those days, there was actually time to comfort those in need, and she had become known for listening intently to those who were suffering — and not just the patients.

One of her ER colleagues was Dimitri, a new cardiologist. They often talked about his unhappy marriage, his wife's constant complaints about his work hours and lack of attention to her, and her propensity for spending. Dimitri, coming from a Greek family that had immigrated to the United States shortly after his eighth birthday, was not accustomed to the fast pace of the city or to the wealth of his wife's New York family.

I realized I already knew a little about Dimitri, because my mother had told me stories of a kind young doctor she worked with. She respected him and felt grateful that he had confided in her. At her wake, he recounted how her compassion and empathy had helped him survive a divorce and move on in constructive ways.

Dimitri managed to go on, but he unfortunately found himself in a world where he never felt quite good enough. As a result, he fell into the trap of believing that money was the evidence of his worth as a person — a stressful trap with dire consequences. A few months ago, I received a call from him. I had not heard from him since my father's funeral fifteen years earlier. He sounded quite tentative as he asked if he could schedule a time to meet with me. I asked what the problem might be, and he replied, "I am about to retire, have been struggling with a lot of stress and not sleeping well, and my wife suggested I talk to someone. Your mother was my first therapist," he kidded. "And now she is gone, so I thought you might be able to help if you have the time."

Dimitri, who is now sixty-eight, has had a very successful career. After his divorce, he remarried and has had a loving but contentious relationship with his wife. Their twin daughters are successful professionals; his youngest son dropped out of college and has yet to find a viable career path. Dimitri is healthy, but he finds aging scary and is particularly worried about not being able to continue to provide for his wife, adult children, grandkids, and extended family.

He told me, "I feel that if I stop working, I will have nothing to give. My wife says I am not a good listener and that I'm always preoccupied, and she is right. I've become an impatient person, and I feel more uneasy than I ever have before in my life. I guess for all these years, I have been the star. I could pay for my kids' private school, tutors, and vacations; I could support my siblings and their families and buy my parents a home on the Cape. Now what will I have to give them if I leave my career? With less money, I am wondering what I will be worth."

One afternoon as we talked, Dimitri began reminiscing about my mother, remembering their debates about whether someone could literally die of a broken heart. He told me she would look at him, smile gently, and say, "Everything is not in books; some things become obvious from living."

He remembered how the doctors loved her and how calm she could be when talking to people in distress. Dimitri recalled, "She was just so good to be with; I am afraid people don't feel that way when they are with me. I am always somewhere else, on to the next project, the next money-making idea, and I never have enough to feel secure."

I commented that I remembered my mother telling me how compassionate he was with patients, how caring he was to the elderly and to her. We talked of how he seemed to undervalue his character and the fact that he is a good person, a good doctor, and a good husband and father, even with his imperfections.

I feel emotional when I meet with Dimitri, not only because he drives one and a half hours every Wednesday afternoon to meet with the son of his first mentor but also because he reminds me of so many stressed people in our current society who are misguided in their quest for peace and happiness. Dimitri, with all his success and money, is not at ease. He is not mentally ill: rather, he has simply lost touch with his inherent goodness. He has bought into an irrational belief system prevalent in our culture — that net worth equals self-worth. As a result, he cannot be fully present with others.

We talked in our last meeting of my mother's lesson to me when my grandfather died. Dimitri wondered if, at the hour of his death, his wife and his adult children would forgive him for his self-absorption, stress, and preoccupation. He asked me, "Who would, if anybody, cry at my funeral?" I answered immediately, "I would." We shared a few tears together.

DIMITRI FINDS HIS WAY

Dimitri asked me one day what he could do to make his wife believe that he could be present to her, not preoccupied and removed. I mentioned that in our couples sessions he reacted to her as she spoke, seemingly listening to a few words and then assuming he understood her meaning, when in fact he consistently missed what she was trying to convey.

He commented, "I think she always wants me to do more, be more; it's demanding, and I always feel like I am failing her."

I responded, "I don't think she is asking for more money or more vacations. I think she is asking you to be fully present, not preoccupied and stressed. Most importantly, she is asking you to listen — to hear what she is saying beyond the surface, to the soft part of her, where her soul resides."

Since that meeting, Dimitri has tried to relate with empathy, calm, and understanding. He has succeeded sometimes, and he has failed sometimes. To his credit, he keeps trying to practice empathic relating — the very thing he respected so much in my mother. In the process, his stress levels have diminished significantly. He is learning how to calm himself and slow his reaction time so that he is able to employ the full benefits of careful listening, creating the kind of emotional connections with other people that he has longed for over many years.

ARE *YOU* LISTENING?

My mother was a brilliantly empathic listener. Dimitri is trying to become a better one. This ability responds to a fundamental need of all human beings, to be listened to and understood. Yet who among us listens more than we talk? When you listen, are you really listening, or are you merely rehearsing what you are going to say when it's your turn to talk? Are you just reloading, planning your response, instead of paying attention? How often do you hear the emotions behind the words and make a genuine effort to address what is unspoken but implied?

More important, how can you learn to listen with compassion and empathy, with the result of reducing stress in yourself and those you are listening to? Below, through stories of some of my clients, I present some of the common challenges to empathic listening and show how it is possible to overcome them.

LEARNING TO HEAR, NOT FIX

I begin each of my group therapy sessions with a focus on empathic listening. At the end of this chapter, I list the same questions that I ask group participants to foster their reflection on what it means to be an empathic listener. If you do the exercises at the end of the chapter, you too will be positioned to become a better listener, and you will likely reduce the tension you are living with in significant, lasting ways.

Listening empathically creates a feeling of trust, which releases the compassionate hormone oxytocin, reducing fear and bias and creating a feeling of security. These brain changes promote open communication, giving us access to conditioned emotional learning and enabling us to restructure distorted thinking and reduce stress.

When you listen, are you picking up certain phrases and ignoring the rest, paying attention only to the good parts of someone's story? Listening seems so easy: you just stop talking and focus on what the other person is saying. Yet of all the skills involved in empathy, listening requires the greatest concentration and focus, for there are so many ways that we can be distracted.

Listening empathically creates a feeling of trust, which releases the compassionate hormone oxytocin, reducing fear and bias and creating a feeling of security.

Many people listen with half an ear, preoccupied and not fully present. We tend to listen with bias, making up our minds before we hear the full story. We listen with sympathy, connecting everything the other person says to our own experiences. We then make well-meaning comments that do not honor the uniqueness of the other person's thoughts or feelings, such as, "I understand exactly what you are feeling," or "I know what you're going through." Finally, we get distracted by the noise of our own internal voices, judging or second-guessing ourselves.

Once our emotions are stimulated, we are far more prone to the cognitive distortions of generalization — thinking that what applies to one situation applies to all situations — and assumed similarity — the tendency to assume that other people hold similar views to our own. For instance, once you get angry at your significant other, the tendency to exaggerate is high. Typical responses might be "You always act like your mother" or "You are stubborn, just like all of your family." Then, in a state of arousal, which blocks rational thought, you may continue assuming that just because you see a situation one way, your partner should automatically agree. Any dissent makes you even angrier.

Cognitive Change

Perceiving a situation from your own perspective is a common distortion that prevents empathic listening and causes defensive reactions in the person who is talking. A change takes place when we slow down and use our innate capacity for empathy to actually listen to the other person's unique expression.

Listening with empathy requires giving up a self-centered view of the world in order to participate fully in another person's experience. It requires focusing and paying attention not only to the words being spoken but also to gestures, body position, and facial expressions. When you listen with empathy, you make a conscious effort to set aside your biases or any distorted thinking you tend to employ. You learn how to connect with the other person's emotions without being carried away by them, to step in and then step back, reading the other person's cues to judge when to move closer and when to give distance. Part of the reason why my mother was such a great empathic listener was that she understood how to live with ambiguity and the inability to find answers or solutions to all problems.

Listening with such clarity and depth of feeling that the other person truly feels "heard" is a kind of holy listening, as the Quaker writer Douglas Steere expresses it in the epigraph to this chapter.[2] Empathic (holy) listening goes deep into the other person's heart and soul to reveal what is hidden by fear, anger, grief, or despair. This kind of listening can be taught. It can be passed from one person to another. We can learn how to listen with empathy by being around people who are empathic and who understand how to "listen our souls into life."

> Empathic (holy) listening goes deep into the other person's heart and soul to reveal what is hidden by fear, anger, grief, or despair.

When we have experienced the power of this kind of listening, we begin to grasp how the ability to listen brings us closer, strengthening our relationships with others and with ourselves. Empathic listening is essentially slow listening, being thoughtful and calm so that we can perceive and express the truth. Empathic interactions change our neurochemistry naturally, without any drug being necessary, to reduce tension, lessen the release of stress hormones, and reduce blood pressure. They expand the lens through which we see the world, producing clear, unbiased thinking and perceiving.

Empathic listening releases the compassion hormone oxytocin, which blocks the release of the stress hormone cortisol. Your brain releases oxytocin when you feel understood and connected to another human being. In addition to reducing stress and preventing the release of cortisol, this neurochemical helps us live longer, promotes calmness, reduces fear and addictive behavior, and increases trust and feelings of security. When we feel calm and secure, we are in a position to correct our distorted thinking.

GAINING AWARENESS OF YOUR STORY

Paul came to one of my recent two-day workshops because he was overwhelmed with stress and struggling with self-consciousness. Two aspects of his life embarrassed him greatly: the blue-collar town he grew up in and the college he attended, which he characterized as mediocre. As the day passed, and as I guided people to listen empathically to him, he began to shed his armor and reveal his embarrassment. After several hours of discussion, Paul realized that his perception of his inferiority was a distorted view he had needlessly carried with him for years.

It is when a person is engaged empathically that neurochemical changes occur. As calming neurochemicals replace stress hormones, tension dissipates. Empathy is now working in two directions: allowing for listening that conveys understanding, and creating accurate perceptions on the part of both the listener and the receiver. Both perceptual and listening abilities are engaged.

Negativity is almost always based on inaccurate interpretations of reality — what CBT therapists call cognitive distortions. As Paul unraveled his negative story, other people examined theirs. One woman talked of not being pretty enough and always feeling anxious to the point of sweating when people looked at her. We helped her see that her perception of herself was not valid. Another woman suffered from stress because of recurrent thoughts that she didn't speak well — not true. A few of the men talked of thinking that their balding hairlines made them unattractive — not true. One man talked of his inferior intelligence, but group consensus also judged this to be not true.

Negativity is almost always based on inaccurate interpretations of reality – what CBT therapists call cognitive distortions.

Whether distortions about ourselves are positive or negative, we must discern the truth in order to remain positive and free of destructive stress. You can't be consistently positive if you're not dealing with reality. The foundation of your sense of self has to be solid and stable. Distortions create road maps that take us to the wrong destination with the wrong people. In Paul's case, empathic listening by other group members enabled him to start addressing his own distortions. Though this process occurs subtly, it is important to recognize, as it demonstrates a link between empathy and CBT. Discerning the truth about yourself or others is not easy, and of course the process depends on who is giving and receiving feedback. In my experience, well-intentioned individuals who commit to providing honest, thoughtful feedback do reach a consensus over time as to the accuracy of any one person's perceptions of another. If five of your closest friends tell you they perceive you as being very stressed lately, it is likely true.

Over years of workshops and group sessions, I have heard stories similar to Paul's repeatedly. The stress caused by negative thinking is profound, and if you don't know where your biases originated, you will remain trapped in the prison of pessimism.

MIND READING

Empathic listening is of fundamental importance in our everyday relationships. Whether you're in a relationship or not, there are insights to be gleaned from this particular context, because the lack of empathic listening can be a source of stress in many contexts.

I have worked with Jess and Michael for several sessions in couples therapy. If you watched a video of our sessions, you would think they had been married only for a year or two. They have not learned as much about each other as you might expect for being married for fifteen years and having two daughters, one in middle school and one in high school.

The stress caused by negative thinking is profound, and if you don't know where your biases originated, you will remain trapped in the prison of pessimism.

When one speaks, the other reveals a facial expression that indicates, "I know exactly what you are going to say," with a knowing look that indicates that the listener is barely paying attention and can't wait to refute whatever is being said. Both are impatient as they anticipate presenting their case, and each is more preoccupied with being right than being loving. As they relate in their typical fashion, I point out the cognitive distortions of *mind reading* and *negatively biased recall*.

Mind reading is a dangerous way of perceiving: it precludes empathy altogether. Rather than using empathy to understand the unique communication of the other, both partners assume they know what the other will say. As a result, they make sweeping assumptions that fuel more conflict and continue the cycle of misunderstanding.

Jess and Michael also engage in negatively biased recall, each of them bringing up every instance of the other's negative behavior while omitting to provide any context for understanding the behavior. Of course, each omits to mention any positive aspect of their history together. This distortion creates much conflict as negatives are highlighted and positive behavior is forgotten or intentionally ignored. The time and situation of a particular comment are not mentioned, as if the offending comment came unexpectedly. Both will reluctantly admit they love one another; their manner of relating, however, drives both of them crazy. They both grew up in homes where this type of relating was typical, and to some degree they both realize they need to unlearn it. Despite their conflicts, their love and attachment to each other brought them to my door.

GETTING YOUR LOVING FROM FIGHTING

With couples who are frequently provoking each other, I often point out how they have wired their brains for fighting. They talk fast, listen poorly, and consistently react from the emotional right hemisphere of the brain. No doubt their blood pressure is elevated, and the stress hormone cortisol, which induces narrow, repetitive thinking, is flooding their brains. This makes them miss all the emotional cues they would observe in one another if they could slow down their reactions and communicate from an empathic perspective.

When couples slow down their interactions and see how stress is distorting their thinking and creating brain overload, they become calmer. They can then begin to discuss the origins of their defeatist behavior patterns and perceive one another more accurately.

For some couples, fighting offers a way of being connected without being vulnerable. People often realize they are being irrational; they will apologize but repeat the pattern again and again without realizing that it can be a form of intimacy, akin to prize fighters who jab at each other all night and then hug at the end of the bout. This kind of sparring creates a flow of adrenaline, which creates a sense of power and righteousness. For an individual who is fragile and views vulnerability as a humiliating state, this can have a protective effect. Fighting is not the only way people cope with the fear of intimacy; joking, avoidance, being too busy, and being preoccupied can also be used to hide dysfunctional beliefs about closeness.

Recently, I met with Peter, a former star college athlete, and his wife, Christine. He came to me because of overwhelming stress, which led to insomnia and a restless state of mind. Peter, who grew up with alcoholic parents, did not receive much empathy or validation as a child. When he gained a lot of weight in middle school, he became the object of teasing and bullying. These early school experiences, along with his dysfunctional home life, led him to see himself as inferior to most of his peers. As he entered high school, he began weightlifting. He was encouraged by coaches to play football, and he eventually found himself in the middle of an offensive line that won the state championship.

Fighting is not the only way people cope with the fear of intimacy; joking, avoidance, being too busy, and being preoccupied can also be used to hide dysfunctional beliefs about closeness.

Despite his athletic success, which earned him a full scholarship to college, Peter's underlying negative view of himself persisted. Christine and Peter married in their senior year of college despite reservations on the part of her parents. They saw Peter as a nervous and uncomfortable man, without a clear plan for his future. His indecisive nature made them doubt his ability to provide for their daughter. Since graduation, he has had trouble finding consistent employment. As his self-esteem has suffered, his stress level has compromised his health. His weight has increased, and he has developed back problems as a result.

Christine contacted me because she had become overly stressed as well, and she felt that their very tense environment was also affecting their two little girls. Peter's stress levels make him preoccupied, and Christine often feels hurt by his lack of affection and inability to be present. Peter, however, has trouble acknowledging her feelings. At the end of one session, he was telling me that he knows how to be intimate, saying, "I have no trouble with that, Doc." As our session had ended, I teased him and asked him to look at Christine directly and give her a kiss as they were leaving my office. Kissing can increase oxytocin, the compassionate hormone, while decreasing cortisol. The same results can occur when romantic partners spend quality time together. Peter became playful with her and started poking her lightly in the arm, pretending to box with her. As they left my office, I saw him pick her up over his shoulder and carry her to their car. He never kissed her, however, nor did he make eye contact without watering down the interaction. He is six feet three inches tall and weighs 265 pounds; she is five feet two inches, yet he was afraid to have an intimate moment with her. This is the reason they came to therapy; she wants more mature love, while he wants her to be happy with his indirect form of love.

> Kissing can increase oxytocin, the compassionate hormone, while decreasing cortisol. The same results can occur when romantic partners spend quality time together.

In subsequent meetings, we focused on Peter's fear of being rejected. Despite being loved by his wife, Peter still falls back on the rejection he experienced as an overweight teen who seldom dated and was often ridiculed. We had to differentiate his past from his present through the use of empathy. With empathy, understanding always precedes explaining. Understanding creates trust; as the emotional door opens to a person's unresolved hurts, it becomes possible to correct entrenched, inaccurate beliefs.

As we progressed in our conversations, Peter became more aware of the unfair distortion he was projecting onto his wife. He had erroneously been wondering, "If women didn't like me back then, how can you find me lovable?" Once he was able to articulate this statement, he became more available in the present. Empathic listening created the safety necessary to let Peter freely express himself and recognize the irrational notions that were guiding his behavior.

The work then began — examining the facts of today. Peter had to begin to finally hear that his wife loved him, that he was free to interact with her spontaneously, and that he would not be rejected. The cognitive distortions of *negative predictions* and *projection* were restructured and placed in the past. A negative prediction is a distortion that overestimates the likelihood that an action will have a negative outcome. Projections are patterns in which we imagine that our own unwanted attributes, thoughts, or emotions are embodied in someone else.

LEARNING TO LISTEN, NOT BLAME

I often ask couples to tell me what it is that they bring to the marriage that makes it so conflictual. I frequently receive answers like "I am impatient, but it's because he always criticizes me," or "Yes, I get angry, but it's because she is so frustrating to live with." In other words, it's not my fault; it's his or hers.

Blaming is one of the most destructive distortions to a marriage or any significant relationship. As long as blaming exists, change cannot occur. Blaming places the need to change on the other person's shoulders and keeps conflict at an impasse.

Both Christine and Peter, the stressed couple I spoke of earlier, work full time; she is a teacher, and he is in sales. They both have significant responsibilities, and they find it difficult to leave the stress of work behind. They are on good behavior at work but tend to save their frustrations for each other. Thus, they are slowly destroying the love they once had.

In a recent session, they complained about each other's dining preferences after attending a play in Boston. Jess wanted to go to the North End for Italian food. Michael thought they had already paid enough for parking, and he finds the restaurants in Boston too crowded and expensive. He wanted to eat closer to home.

They headed out of the city; she pouted, and he became angry with her for withdrawing. He then drove fast and made her uncomfortable with his impatience behind the wheel. When they discussed this occurrence in my office, neither could wait to tell me their side of the story. They were both highly reactive and trying to convince me of their innocence and of the other's wrongdoing. A minor issue became a mood changer. They were both tired and depleted that night in my office, and each held the other responsible for the misery and excessive stress they were feeling.

Rather than accept responsibility for their own deficits, both Christine and Peter projected blame. Ironically, they would both deny this tendency and say it is the style of the other; but it is a way of relating that they share. Many couples struggle with the inability to admit and acknowledge mistakes. It seems easier for a fragile ego to blame and accuse others of causing unhappiness. I often say to such couples that they would likely have the same difficulties no matter whom they married. Blamers develop the tendency to project onto others what they deny in themselves years before they ever marry. This dynamic will erode love in any relationship. Often those who project blame are unaware that the fault they criticize in their spouse is their own deficit.

Blamers develop the tendency to project onto others what they deny in themselves years before they ever marry.

This tendency often has roots in early experience. If you are treated with care and respect for your uniqueness, you learn to handle difficult emotions and become socially competent. If, however, you are neglected, ignored, criticized, or mistreated, you are more likely to defend your shaky sense of self. You learn to blame others, become obsessed with perfection, project your thoughts and feelings onto others, and practice intolerance, all of which can lead to a host of negative emotions like anger, hostility, resentment, fear, shame, and guilt.

I can tell when I first meet a couple how they will fare based on each partner's ability to understand the other's perspective and their ability to accept and take responsibility for the difficulties in their own relational style. The stress of our fast-paced culture and our competitive working environment has made couples like Peter and Christine even less likely to learn how to maintain intimacy. They are both competitors: they compete successfully at work, and they compete with each other over who is right and wrong. Neither exercises regularly; they eat poorly; both are overweight and do not sleep nearly enough to counteract the level of stress they endure daily. As a result, they have little patience for each other. The thought of changing their lifestyle is a threat to both their egos, so they are resistant to change. When they look to each other to soothe their tension, they become frustrated and disappointed. Then the blame game starts all over again. Couples sessions often begin this way, as accumulated hurts have hidden any positive views that the partners might have of each other.

So Christine and Peter bark at each other; they talk at each other, their voices raised, their spirits depleted, as they battle to protect their viewpoints with the little remaining energy they have each night. The stress they produce affects their digestion, their sex drive, and their immune systems. It causes tension headaches and contributes to their weight gain as well. Unfortunately, these effects of stress are not uncommon among couples in our society.

Cognitive Change

In order to break the cycle this couple is stuck in, I have to get them to slow down their reaction time so that they can listen to one another without becoming defensive. I monitor who is speaking, which calms them both in my presence, and I don't allow either one to interrupt the other. They voice their complaints, and we examine each one to assess the facts without high emotion. I am asking them to use the brain's thoughtful left hemisphere. I explain how they have been ruled by the *microsecond reactions* of the emotional brain. As they slow down and become more thoughtful, their stress dissipates, and their answers become more realistic. The distortions of the past seem to fade gradually. Through our sessions, they are learning how to control the emotional brain and limit its domination of their thinking. I am essentially training them to be empathic — to enter into each other's soul rather than defending and criticizing. Any couple who are motivated to understand one another rather than always being motivated to prove themselves in the right can implement these steps. They then have access to a stress-reduction technique they can employ at any time, in any situation.

QUIETING THE ADVICE GIVER

Empathic listening takes practice and an understanding of our own tendencies to react to someone else's story. In a workshop focused on empathy training to uncover conditioned learning and reduce stress, Larry began talking about his conflict with his recently deceased mother, whom he described as overly critical. He told us he felt guilty about her death because they never resolved their differences. He has been left wishing he could have expressed himself more openly to her. Larry's stress level has increased since his mother's funeral. As an only child, he imagines that relatives are critical of him for not visiting his mother more often.

As he continued to speak, another group member, Lynn, an overly stressed salesperson, started to give Larry unsolicited advice, based on her experience after the death of her own mother a year earlier. It was obvious that she was interrupting the flow of his speech, and he looked as though he was trying to mask his irritation.

As he recoiled, she kept talking, offering more guidance, and it was apparent that he was not taking in her suggestion to let go of the past and adopt a new view. At one point, he asked Lynn if she had a difficult time with his emotions; she said no but kept talking and offering more suggestions, missing the message he was trying to deliver. I encouraged him to speak out to Lynn rather than withdraw as he did when he felt misunderstood by his mother. He told Lynn he knew she was trying to help but that she seemed so reactive, intent on stopping him from feeling, "like you want to fix me but can't hear me."

She sank back into her chair and then went on to tell Larry that she was the kid criticized like he was, left alone to figure out why her mother was so very angry at her so often. She continued, "The only thing I knew how to do was to sing a song to myself and tune her out. I made myself go forward." The only problem with Lynn's efforts to go forward is that she seldom allows herself or others to feel the depth of emotion that rightly accompanies certain situations.

One group member was confused by the discussion and asked, "How do we change our story? Should we feel more, move past the hurts of yesterday, tell the story over and over again until we can get past it, or what?" My answer was that we change in the moment, but not simply by telling our story repetitively. Larry is changing because he addressed a dominant woman differently than he would have addressed his mother. Instead of withdrawing in anger, he slowed Lynn down so that she could hear him, and he could hear her. As a result of his ability to calm the interaction, they increased their understanding of each other. Larry regulated the temperature in a way that he previously would not have been able to do. Instead of repeating yesterday's story, he rewrote the ending by taking a healthy action in the present. He spoke to Lynn calmly, and his tone of voice conveyed how much he wanted to convey his genuine desire to understand her. Lynn seemed touched, and rather than being defensive as she would have been previously, received his feedback and accepted the reality check he and others gave her. Together, through mutual empathic listening, they danced in sync. Empathy goes out the window if the environment is too hot or too cold; being angry or detached limits empathy.

> Empathy goes out the window if the environment is too hot or too cold; being angry or detached limits empathy.

Cognitive Change

Larry and Lynn made a cognitive change through an interaction that evolved from the right hemisphere of the brain to the left, from automatic thoughts to realistic thoughts. They shifted from the distortions of *personalizing* — taking something personally that may not be personal — and *assumed similarities* — the tendency to assume that other people hold similar attitudes to your own — to employing empathic listening to perceive the truth and reach a desired outcome based on mutual understanding. A cognitive change has taken place. Their brains are now producing calming neurochemicals, and they can begin to use the fact-oriented capacity of empathy to discern and express the truth. Let's continue to explore some practical ways to improve communication and express empathy.

OVERCOMING SELF-ABSORPTION

One of the most profound hindrances to quality relationships is self-absorption. In my workshops, I can only imagine how bored people sometimes are as they listen to others go on in dramatic fashion about themselves. Some of the speakers don't even read the cues of the disenchanted faces right in front of them. To become an empathic listener, you can learn by paying attention to the people who listen to you. When you are speaking, look at the person, or persons, you are addressing. If you want to know whether what you're saying is interesting, all the feedback you need is there in the faces and the body language of your listeners. When you call someone on the phone, ask the other person if it's a good time to talk. Don't assume that they've been waiting to hear from you. While you're talking on the phone, check in with the listener to see how that person perceives you. Ask questions like, "Do you want me to go on? What do you think of what I just said?" Of course there are people whom you will not be interested using your energy to listen to intently. With empathy as a guide, we learn to read others better, and we are more prepared to decide which individuals we want to invest in — whom to get closer to and whom to remain distant from.

ENTITLEMENT BELIEFS: I TALK, YOU LISTEN

People with narcissistic tendencies seldom realize they could say what they mean with far fewer words. Their need to be at the center of a conversation tends to make them long-winded. Remember, whether you are writing or speaking, fewer words with clear meaning are more appealing. If you traditionally talk more than you listen, you're cutting off the potential for an empathic interchange. Conversely, it's not empathic to just listen to someone go on and on, all the while saying to yourself, "Does she have any idea she told me this all before?" Being passive with someone who is narcissistic is not empathic, and it creates internal stress for the listener. If the speaker characteristically does not come up for air, it is empathic to interrupt and say, "I really don't like interrupting, but I don't think you realize that you already told me this story." You are giving the person truthful feedback in a tactful way: that is empathic. Narcissistic people need feedback, and most often, they probably don't receive it, because they tend to be fragile and defensive. As a result, people often avoid telling them the truth. You may be surprised to find that if you're tactful — and your intention is not to be hurtful — your feedback may be received gratefully.

Empathic conversations involve give-and-take. My grandfather did not care about meaningful dialogue in his talks over the dinner table with my mother. He always talked about his business ventures, while she listened. Ask yourself if your interactions with others seem to be balanced, or whether one party dominates the dialogue. Ask yourself whether you are truly interested in the person you're talking to, or whether you are just looking to get something for yourself. If you know how to listen and give of yourself, you will always attract people; it never fails.

FRAGILE SELF-WORTH

In the early part of my career, I worked with patients who were seriously disturbed and could fit the classification of mentally ill. Over time, my focus changed, and I began receiving referrals for people who were clearly not mentally ill, and in fact embodied many of the qualities that are highly regarded in professional and public life. Not only did they have mastery over practical skills, but they also demonstrated attitudes and abilities that distinguished them as extraordinarily competent. Most often these individuals came to me because they had difficulty maintaining intimacy, difficulty being present, and in essence difficulty being empathic. They had lost their souls in the pursuit of image, status, and material wealth. They had achieved success on the outside at the cost of chronic stress and discomfort on the inside.

> Ask yourself if your interactions with others seem to be balanced, or whether one party dominates the dialogue. Ask yourself whether you are truly interested in the person you're talking to, or whether you are just looking to get something for yourself.

Dimitri, my mother's colleague, is an excellent example of how achievement and status can change an individual. If your self-worth can be easily tarnished, if you grew up feeling "not good enough," and if you are a capable human being, it is easy to lose your bearings in our fast-paced world of competition and greed. Our culture is dominated by the collective compulsion to succeed regardless of the personal cost, causing estrangement from family and friends as well as ill health. Dimitri, who once possessed an expansive empathic range, became a man addicted to achievement, not realizing that his regard for people was withering — and most important, that he was losing his regard for himself.

My life's work for the last several years has been to try to understand why people with glowing credentials, a fine education, and often significant wealth do not feel good about themselves and, as a result, are not in a position to do much good for others. I spend hours weekly with corporate CEOs, CFOs, project managers, attorneys, physicians, scientists, engineers, accountants, financial advisers, lobbyists, media personnel, and professional athletes. In essence, these are good people who have lost their way, lost their souls, and don't know how to retrieve the good feeling they once had about themselves. They have little insight into the benefits that empathic listening and accurate perceiving can provide — for them as well as for others. Their misguided beliefs and inability to slow down and enter another person's world have created a void in their adult lives. We can learn from their mistakes by adopting a mindset of empathic relating to others.

THE DOING BEGINS

Now it's time to complement your newfound knowledge about empathic listening with action. Don't rush, as the learning will be compromised if you do. These assignments may seem like a lot of work, but it is important work: we all need accountability to others and ourselves to make progress. Each of us is too subjective to clarify our thinking alone. To maximize the benefits of these exercises, try to tune in to a place within you where calm energy resides. Just by doing that, you are changing your neurochemistry and starting to reduce your stress. Every thought you have is accompanied by a neurochemical reaction. A calm mood elicits calm chemicals, allowing your brain to store information that will easily be recalled.

Empathy training consists of two main factors: *empathic listening* and *expressing empathy*.

Empathic Listening

This exercise can be practiced either through role playing with friends and family members or by applying the concepts in real life.

Try practicing the following aspects of empathic listening:

- **reflective listening** (repeating what the person says)
- **rephrasing content** in your own words (trying to understand the speaker by summarizing what you have heard)
- **emphasizing what the person feels** (rephrasing the content and reflecting the feeling); *showing genuine interest* in the speaker
- **paying attention to body language** (not sympathizing but instead focusing on the unique expression of the speaker)
- **limiting identifying and generalizing**, being judgmental or critical, lecturing, advising, or interrupting

Try to use statements that invite the speaker to expand on his or her thoughts, such as:

- I feel...
- It seems like...
- As I understand it, you sound...
- It appears as if...
- If I hear you correctly, you'd like...
- I notice...
- I imagine that feels...
- Tell me more about that...
- Are you saying that...?

Expressing Empathy

Learning how to express empathy — putting your thoughts and feelings into words that find their way into another person's heart and soul — requires self-awareness, careful reflection, and a considerable amount of practice. To help people learn how to express their insights in ways that help rather than hurt, I have devised the following guidelines:

- **Ask open-ended questions.** This puts preconceptions aside while expressing true interest in the other person's perspective. Instead of asking your teenage daughter, "Honey, do you really think your date was cute?" you might ask, "How was your evening with your new date?"
- **Slow down.** Empathy slows things down so that emotions can be tempered with thoughtful reflection.
- **Avoid snap judgments.** Empathy does not categorize based on past experience but sees human beings as always changing and evolving.
- **Pay attention to your body and the other person's.** Empathy is an integrated mind-body response; thoughts interact with feelings in an empathetic nervous-system response. Physiological empathy is a give-and-take process: through mirroring each other's nervous systems, we exchange much-needed information.
- **Learn from the past.** We need to understand our past so that our theories and old patterns do not interfere with understanding and perceiving. If you are unaware of your own biases from the past, your ability to perceive accurately will be compromised. For instance, if you have a fear of anger because your father had a short temper, you may be overly sensitive to people you encounter who are passionate but not angry.
- **Let the story unfold.** Every person's story needs to proceed at its own pace. With empathy, we can judge with surprising accuracy how fast or slow the other person needs to go; timing is everything.

- **Set boundaries.** Empathy suffers if the listener's emotions become confused with those of the speaker; it requires objectivity. If you feel too close to the situation — for example, if what the person is describing reminds you of an emotional situation that occurred in your life — you can become overly identified with the other person's problems and you can lose your objectivity. Once you become aware of this situation, try to slow down and try to put aside your past experiences so that you can truly listen with fresh ears rather than from the limited and often misguided perspective of identifying with another's experience too closely.

Questions to Answer

Try to use the principles of empathic listening and expressing empathy in answering the following questions:

- Can you give an example of an open-ended question?
- What techniques can you use to calm yourself so you can listen attentively?
- Do you notice how calm, empathic listening lessens stress? Can you specify how you feel when you have been able to listen empathically?
- Can you give an example of how you have employed reflective listening, and how you have been able to rephrase the content of an interaction so that a person feels understood?
- Can you give an example of an interaction where you have avoided categorizing and have demonstrated an open mind?
- Can you specify a time where you were tempted to talk about yourself but asked questions instead, and noticed

the other person actually revealed more about himself or herself?

Recognizing Cognitive Distortions

We have identified eight cognitive distortions that can significantly affect our relationships:

- blaming
- mind reading
- negatively biased recall
- negative predictions
- projecting
- microsecond reactions
- personalizing
- assumed similarities

From the stories in this chapter, what triggers can you identify that cause you to employ cognitive distortions? How can you limit your use of these distortions?

Create a log with statements containing cognitive distortions listed on the left side and restructured statements on the right side. Note every time you have used one of these distortions, calm yourself, and then restructure your original statement into a truthful, fact-oriented statement. Make as many comments as you deem necessary for each distortion. Do this exercise every day for two consecutive weeks.

BLAMING STATEMENT	RESTRUCTURED STATEMENT
So I come in late every now and then. My boss should just let it go instead of complaining.	I have been late on several occasions. I need to take responsibility for my tardiness and arrive on time.
MIND-READING STATEMENT	RESTRUCTURED STATEMENT
I know she doesn't like me; she was frowning when she passed by my desk this morning.	I have no idea what she was thinking when she passed by my desk; she was frowning, but she could have a headache or be preoccupied with some other matter.

Repeat for each form of cognitive distortion.

Take Action

Make a contract with someone very close to you to give each other truthful feedback in person or electronically every day for one week as to the quality of your listening. Commit to be open to feedback and to asking how you can improve so that you both make progress together. Note your experience in your journal.

CHAPTER 4

The Soul's Pharmacy
How to Produce Calming Neurochemicals

Everyone feels at ease and safe around those who cherish others.

THUBTEN CHODRON, *An Open-Hearted Life*

My mother never went to high school, but she possessed a natural ability to diagnose an emotional problem and provide exactly the remedy that was needed. In her presence, I always felt calm. She knew how to soothe agitation and discomfort and replace them with energy and a sense of wellness. As I was growing up, I never questioned why my mother had this effect on me and others: it was simply a given. Not until I was a doctoral candidate at the University of Massachusetts did I begin to understand that my mother embodied the soul of a psychologist.

During this time I had a Siberian husky puppy, who came to me after a three-month stay in a pet store. Kima had been traumatized by the experience of being taken from her mother and transferred to a cramped cage in a cold and threatening environment. No matter what I tried, I could not soothe her fears. She spent most of her time trembling underneath my bed. Finally, feeling overwhelmed, I decided to take Kima to see my mother. I hoped that her soothing manner would provide comfort to my stressed pet.

When we arrived at my mother's house, Kima immediately headed for the bedroom and hid under the bed. No amount of coaxing could bring her out. I spent a relaxing evening with my parents and eventually went to bed myself, hoping that Kima would feel less scared the next day.

I woke in the morning, refreshed, and I could hear the sound of my mother's voice from the den. Looking inside, I saw my mother stretched out on the sofa, with Kima nestled serenely against her chest. My mother was stroking Kima and speaking to her in a quiet voice.

I couldn't believe my eyes. I asked my mother what had happened, and she replied simply, "We made a relationship."

"Have you been up all night?" I asked. She nodded, as if it were nothing. I saw that she did not look the least bit tired. In fact, she looked invigorated.

After that day, Kima was transformed. It was as if all her fears had been wiped away by my mother's touch. I didn't question this result, or how it had come about, but when I later mentioned it to my psychology professor, he was fascinated. When I added that I always felt calm in my mother's presence, and that she had this remarkable effect on other people too, he nodded thoughtfully. "Your neurochemistry changes when you are with her," he said. "It's not just that you feel calmer. You *are* calmer."

When I said that I also felt stronger and more energized after being with my mother, his eyes lit up. "Of course," he said. "Your neurochemistry interacts with the other aspects of your physiology."

At the time, the notion seemed radical. There was little research that showed an actual physiological connection between mind and body. Today, we have an impressive body of scientific research demonstrating that our beliefs, attitudes, and emotions have a direct effect on our physical well-being. They are factors in our susceptibility to disease and our ability to recover, and they may be the key to healthy aging, longevity, and a stress-free life.

Over the years I consciously incorporated the lesson I learned from my mother into my clinical practice, and this is what I discovered:

- A simple human interaction can change your neuro-chemistry.
- A change in your neurochemistry can trigger a change in your body.

This understanding became the foundation of my work, along with the realization that empathy provides the foundation for positive neurochemical changes. My mother knew how to read people and animals so that she could provide what they needed to feel safe and secure. She created conditions that allowed others to develop openness and a sense of calm. What my mother called "making a relationship" was a powerful method of healing both the mind and the body while producing the resiliency to cope with the stressors of life. You can practice this method by following the guidelines on expressing empathy at the conclusion of chapter 3.

When we slow down and use empathy to observe another person without preconceived notions, we can begin to sense what that person needs to feel safe and understood. We have established a foundation for honest, reciprocal communication.

> When we slow down and use empathy to observe another person without preconceived notions, we can begin to sense what that person needs to feel safe and understood. We have established a foundation for honest, reciprocal communication.

THE TAKEAWAY

What behaviors did my mother exemplify that you can duplicate? The most important gift she gave my little puppy was one that is often not valued in our current culture: she gave her *time*, and she gave her time *unselfishly*. In order to do this, we have to slow down, let go of our own preoccupations, and become present in the moment.

My mother also used her empathy to see beyond the surface. For instance, my father ignored the puppy, thinking Kima just wanted to be alone. My mother understood that the dog was afraid to be approached, not that she didn't want to be comforted. She eased her way into Kima's heart and calmed her. We benefit when we take the time to see beyond the obvious. For instance, people who seem aloof are often shy, people who are angry are often hurt, and people who act guilty are often exaggerating their importance (they assume that if they don't do what others expect, people will be overly affected). To lessen your stress and the stress in other people, try to avoid jumping to conclusions about the motivations behind their behavior. Ask yourself if you're taking the time to see beyond the surface.

To use this approach to reduce stress and relate successfully to others, you need to spend time with people engaging in the same practice of expressing and receiving empathy, and changing cognitive distortions and the schemas they support.

People we relate to know when we are somewhere else in our minds and whether we are employing empathic listening to truly try and understand them. As you're reading these lines, you're probably saying to yourself, "Sure, easy to say, very hard to do." In the modern world, it is in fact very difficult to slow down, to leave our smartphones and become totally available to other people. To use this approach to reduce stress and relate successfully to others, you need to spend time with people engaging in the same practice of expressing and receiving empathy, and changing cognitive distortions and the schemas they support. Group therapy, support groups, and groups of friends with the same relationship goals are all helpful in making the transition to perceiving accurately. Share your goals in this regard with those close to you, ask them to engage with you in the process, and, if possible, share the guidelines in this book with them.

MIND AND BODY AS ONE

The connection between mind and body, the dynamic interplay between mental processes and our physiology, has been amply documented by an expanding body of scientific research. Mental health is no longer viewed in isolation from our other bodily processes. We are integrated beings.

With our growing understanding of this connection, we can learn to manage our mind-body pathways to maximize our health and reduce stress. We can let go of the misconception that we are born with specific, unalterable personality traits and instead become the people we want to be. Dr. Daniel Siegel, director of the Center for Human Development in Los Angeles, has shown with numerous studies that humans are not the victims of some grand genetic puppet master. Although he acknowledges that genes play an important role in our lives, he emphasizes that our experiences influence the expression of our genes and the way the brain is organized.[1]

Moreover, development continues throughout life. We're not stuck with the negative impulses we may experience at any given point in our lives. Rather, close emotional relationships continue to influence us throughout our lives, constantly providing opportunities to change the circuitry of our brains that controls our behavioral impulses, our emotions, and our tendencies to feel stressed, anxious, or calm. The brain's ability to reorganize itself by forming new neural connections is called *neuroplasticity*. This is what enables us to recognize and change the cognitive distortions we have been conditioned to use and begin to see ourselves and others clearly.

This research has exciting implications for our overall health, longevity, and state of mind. Psychotherapists and their clients can use the tools of science to produce results that never before seemed possible. Today, when we talk about brain chemistry, we are aware that a change in neurochemistry sends signals to all parts of the body. For example, it is widely accepted by medical scientists that our attitudes, moods, and behaviors can affect our immune systems both negatively and positively, making us more or less susceptible to infectious illnesses and diseases like cancer. Likewise, numerous studies have demonstrated that anger, hostility, resentment, isolation, and other stresses are important risk factors for heart disease. A reduction in stress is a key factor in preventing heart attacks.

A growing body of research also shows that both longevity and quality of life are strongly influenced by our relationships. The longest continuous study of physical and mental health, conducted by the Department of Psychiatry at Harvard Medical School, has concluded that relationship factors are among the key predictors of successful aging. The study, which has tracked the lives of 237 (male) Harvard students since 1937 and was later expanded to study a group of inner-city disadvantaged youths as well, concludes that most of the factors that predict health and happiness are within an individual's control, even when they lack social advantages, high income, or high job status.[2] Dr. George Vaillant, who has directed the study from its inception, has identified seven factors that predict healthy, low-stress aging. The three most significant are:

- having a good marriage before the age of fifty
- possessing the resilience to cope with difficult situations
- expressing altruistic behavior

The list includes no factors beyond an individual's control, such as social class or genetic risk for disease. Essentially, the keys to a healthy life are knowing how to manage stress and how to form lasting, quality relationships. Dr. Vaillant emphasizes that these abilities can be learned: we can change our coping styles and the way we relate to other people with disciplined efforts and therapy. He believes a successful old age depends more on our efforts than on our genes. Our ability to manage our neurochemistry becomes key to living happily and with as little stress as possible.

As our understanding of neuroplasticity grows, we are seeing confirmation that it can also be used to remedy neurological conditions once thought impossible to treat except with pharmaceuticals, as if the brain were a muscle that grows stronger when it is worked. Researchers at the UCLA Medical School found that patients with obsessive-compulsive disorder (OCD) who changed their behavior by not giving in to urges repeatedly showed a decrease in brain activity associated with the obsessive-compulsive urges.[3] They were, in effect, changing their neurochemistry naturally. I have seen this change occur in patients with OCD: for example, they have been able to overcome their embarrassment about being obsessive first through experiencing understanding and acceptance of their behavior and then undoing the cognitive distortions that support continued OCD, such as catastrophizing and emotional reasoning.

New research on fetal stem cells indicates that neurons can regenerate. Brains damaged by Parkinson's, Alzheimer's, and stroke might actually be capable of producing new brain cells to fill the roles of cells that have died. While most neurons cannot regrow, in a few specific regions, such as the hippocampus, the birth and differentiation of neurons continues throughout life.

Imagine the potential if we choose to harness our natural abilities, both behavioral and physiological, to grow and thrive.

DIM THE LIGHTS

So how do we bring about these beneficial changes in our brain organization and chemistry? Learning how to create a calm, balanced state of mind often helps you regulate your neurochemical state without antidepressants or antianxiety agents. The effect in your brain is like a dimmer switch in a room, lowering the light when it is not needed. We need to be able to turn down the dial on our emotions when intensity is not needed or productive, saving our energy for situations that demand it. In the process, we produce the calming neurochemicals serotonin and oxytocin, paving the way for stress reduction and increased happiness. Serotonin controls anger and impulsiveness and helps balance mood. Oxytocin, the hormone of compassion, reduces anxiety, promotes calmness, lessens addictive cravings, increases trust, and reduces fear. In addition, loving connections stimulate the vagus nerve, which regulates heart rhythms. It also promotes better regulation of glucose and immune system function while releasing additional oxytocin. This sequence of neural activity can be stimulated even by casual encounters with coworkers, acquaintances, and the man who takes your order for coffee at your morning breakfast place.

Learning how to create a calm, balanced state of mind often helps you regulate your neurochemical state without antidepressants or antianxiety agents.

These hormones are particularly effective in reducing the release of the stress hormone cortisol, thus creating a sense of calm and a reduction in stress.

JOURNAL QUESTIONS

Awareness is key to stimulating feel-good neurochemicals. Examine your responses to stress with the following questions:

- Do you have a dimmer switch in your arsenal of coping mechanisms?
- If not, how will you develop the ability to calm down when you are under stress? What actions will you take?
- In what ways does your body tell you that you are under stress?

- What are the typical situations that trigger a stressful reaction for you?
- How can you reprogram your brain to cope with these typical stressors?

In addition, to keep a regular inventory of the quality of your interactions, please answer the following questions daily:

- How often did you feel in tune with those you encountered?
- How often did you really listen, smile, and make consistent eye contact?

TAKE ACTION

In addition to evaluating your own emotions, get feedback from those close to you. Ask them if they think you are really present during conversations. Over the course of a week, ask at least five individuals you encountered for a significant amount of time for feedback as to how calm or anxious they felt in your presence.

Each of these tasks is related to regulating your chemical balance. Performing them regularly and recording the answers can increase positive emotions and stimulate vagus nerve activity.

CHAPTER 5

The Illusions We Create
Seeing More Clearly with CBT

Truth is too simple for us. We do not like those who
unmask our illusions.

RALPH WALDO EMERSON, "Truth," 1861

In many ways, empathy is synonymous with objectivity, which is defined as seeing the world as it is, realistically, without distortion. It is only when we see the true essence of another human being and they see us in the same way that love can flourish.

When we fail to see others and ourselves clearly, we are usually pulled back to what I call the scene of the crime — the unresolved mysteries of the past that continue to blind our perceptions in the present.

My clients are my greatest teachers, and my client John's story is a poignant example of how illusions create unnecessary stress and suffering.

A few weeks ago, John, who seldom drinks, had one too many. After a stressful sales quarter, he did not make his quota, and his bonus was significantly affected. He drove home in an unsteady state and was arrested for drunk driving.

John is an intense man. He is absorbed in his work in software sales. He is seldom able to be present in a way that makes people feel he is listening and comprehending: he has often been accused of being too self-absorbed. In essence, his empathic abilities are lacking. He also has a history of feeling overly anxious. His mental state had become completely dependent on his sales numbers in each quarter. But his sales and his income are volatile: he has had years when he made over $200,000, and years where he made less than $80,000. A few weeks after his arrest he was notified that he had failed to make his sales quota for the second straight quarter, and he was laid off. He was feeling humiliated and ashamed, which are common emotional states for those who find it difficult to manage the stress of success.

John is a decent person, but one who is profoundly misdirected in his efforts to live a happy, fulfilled life. His father was accomplished in the business world. His mother worked full time as an administrative assistant, and together they provided a secure upbringing for him and his sister. Neither parent was particularly attuned to their children; John describes them both as poor listeners, preoccupied with their own interests. You can understand how he emerged with the mindset of providing financially but not attending to the emotional needs of those close to him — a *core belief* system that has led to chronic stress and unhappiness.

As we talked, he became more aware of his core beliefs, and particularly his tendency to use the cognitive distortion of *catastrophizing* — thinking of unpleasant events as catastrophes because they fall short of expectations.

At one point John and his wife separated: she could not tolerate the constant stress he brought to their home. She thought a separation would motivate him to change his ways and learn how to calm himself. She tried to get him to understand that this would be a good change for him and their family.

He always thought of his wife as staying with him for pragmatic reasons. "I gave her a comfortable life; I'm not sure she would have stayed with me if I didn't work so hard, make the big bucks." He talks about his adult daughter in the same terms. "I didn't attend many of her sporting events, but I was always there to pay for a fancy vacation. I let her buy expensive clothes, bought her a great car in high school, and sent her to an expensive private college. She didn't have to borrow a cent." Because his daughter was in the middle of planning an expensive wedding when John lost his job, he hadn't even told her that he had been laid off, fearing her disappointment.

John has related to me in a similar fashion, often making jokes about paying me and asking if I would still help him if he had no money. "Would you cast me to the curb, Doc?"

GIVING AND RECEIVING EMPATHY

Poignantly, since John's DUI arrest, he has experienced a depth of love based on empathy and compassion that he had never been open to feeling before. He could not believe how much his wife missed him when they separated. He thought for sure that she was seeking a divorce and had only told him it was a temporary separation to break the news to him slowly. He thought she no longer loved him.

As John and I developed trust, he became more willing to work on his problematic thinking pattern of *mind reading* and *ignoring the positive*. He began to understand the value of empathic listening to help him perceive accurately what others are expressing to him. Quick reactors often perceive incorrectly, neglecting to take the time necessary to assess the meaning of another person's communication. John eventually gained control over his overly rapid interpretation of the content and emotions of a conversation by practicing slowing down as he engaged his wife and daughter.

He commented on feeling calmer in our interactions and in his relationships. He was feeling better not only because he was receiving empathy but also because he was learning how to give empathy to others. This reciprocal process led to less stress and stronger connections with the people who mattered the most to him. He extended the empathic resonance between us to his wife and family. He finally realized that his wife's love was undeniable, as he saw in her eyes how very much she cared and how devastated she was at seeing him so stressed and unhappy. He was amazed that his daughter came to him when she learned of his troubles and pleaded with him to let her cancel the elaborate wedding plans. To reduce the pressure on him, she had already begun changing the plan to a smaller and simpler occasion with just extended family and a few friends. He was so emotionally moved that I extended my workday on several occasions to meet with him and his family.

John's self-absorption began to melt in the face of overpowering empathy. He has developed a softer, more attentive presence, with the capacity to give and receive empathy. He appears to have discovered a much-sought-after level of intimacy. He has been longing for years to feel loved for who he is, not just for what he provides. He knows now that his rapid judgments and constant need for action were fruitless efforts to win love. John is certainly not out of the woods, but he does have a much clearer idea of what brings love. Empathic giving and receiving is surely a key.

HIGH EXPECTATIONS/HIGH STRESS

Expectations drive desire and hope. However, expecting to correct an emotional deficit with a positive accomplishment leads to disappointment and chronic stress. Expectations are caused by a natural yearning to actualize one's potential. On a deeper level, expectations can create a conditioned belief as to what behaviors or accomplishments you think will bring you love and boost your sense of self. Your *core beliefs* about the factors that you think will lead to success reveal what your expectations are made of and what you consciously or unconsciously believe will produce the desired outcomes.

Expectations lift our spirits and excite us neurochemically, producing the feel-good chemical dopamine. Neuroscientists call this
response *expectation anticipation*. Anticipation triggers the release of dopamine. Expectations can also,
however, depress our spirits and trigger the release
of negative neurochemicals if, rather than being
based on the desire to actualize potential, they are
actually efforts to overcome the wounds of childhood. Successful outcomes bring fleeting joy, and
disappointments bring an exaggerated feeling of
failure, eliciting stress hormones.

Many driven people do not realize that their
real quest is not money or possessions but a deeper
desire to finally feel worthy. We must understand

> Expectations
> drive desire and
> hope. However,
> expecting to
> correct an
> emotional
> deficit with
> a positive
> accomplishment
> leads to
> disappointment
> and chronic
> stress.

that expectations fuel our spirit, but the achievement of a goal will
lose its significance over time, especially if our hidden agenda is to
heal unresolved hurts from the past.

Our minds naturally try to figure out ways of measuring our
success or failure. In our culture, we are stressed and obsessed with
competition and markers of worth. One of the common ways of
assessing success is to place a number on our efforts. For instance,
salespeople like John frequently talk of making or not making their
quota. As John desperately tried to meet his quota, he became locked
in a cycle of negative emotions and fruitless behaviors. He was com-
pulsively looking to the number for indications of how worthy he
was on any given day. And his obsession with numbers didn't stop
at work. The square footage of his home, his weight, his age, the
value of his retirement fund, the weight he could bench-press, and
the accumulation of vacation days he didn't use all became markers
of where he stood in relation to others.

Depending on the significance a person attaches to these
measures of success, the results of failing to meet a goal can be

devastating. John, for instance, had surges of dopamine daily, if not hourly, as his computer regularly told him where he stood in relation to his peers. His mood would go up or down depending on how close he was to achieving his sales goal, which is a highly stressful way to live. Unfortunately, he didn't realize that he was attempting to solve his internal problem with an external solution. This is a mistake common among stressed high achievers.

> Many driven people do not realize that their real quest is not money or possessions but a deeper desire to finally feel worthy.

John knows today that his quest to reach the perfect number brought him only short-term success. When he was making $200,000 a year, he was no happier than when he made $80,000. Sure, at first he felt elevated, and the number soothed his fragile sense of self. As time went on, however, his typical mood returned. Psychologists refer to the phenomenon of *hedonic adaptation*, meaning that we generally have a set point (or "thermostat") for happiness. Our happiness level may spike or plunge in response to a change in our lives, but eventually we settle back into our typical level of happiness with the changed situation. Lottery winners are ecstatic initially, but eventually they return to their previous level of happiness. In fact, they have higher levels of depression than the general population.

John learned over time that he was operating with a mythical *belief system*. He believed that people would love and respect him if he increased his status in life, made more money, or bought a bigger house. His belief system, common to our culture, was so embedded in his psyche that when he did poorly at work and was arrested, he perceived these events as proof that he was worthless and believed his family would be better off without him.

Changing a story you have created and lived by for many years is incredibly difficult, but in John's case, the love of his family at his darkest moments was more powerful than his lifelong convictions.

He was vulnerable, weak, and frightened. As a result he became more open and genuine, and his family felt closer to him, and he felt closer to them. The give-and-take of empathy provided the foundation necessary for John to examine his core beliefs and the cognitive distortions he had been living by. He found the way to lasting love through his suffering, not through his accomplishments. We all suffer in life, but those who suffer and learn are far happier and less stressed than those who suffer and blame.

EMPATHY BEGINS THE PROCESS OF CHANGING A NEGATIVE STORY

John has experienced the profound, life-changing effects of one person's providing empathic attunement to another. He has realized the value of in-depth relating and learned how mutual empathy sets the stage for perceiving the truth about oneself and others. As a result, his tendency toward self-absorption has decreased markedly. He is committed to being more available to his family and friends, without the old tendency to drift away into his own world.

> We all suffer in life, but those who suffer and learn are far happier and less stressed than those who suffer and blame.

John's belief that performance will bring love and respect is part of a cultural dynamic that I call *performance addiction:* the belief that perfecting your appearance and increasing your social or professional status will secure love, respect, and happiness. It is extremely common in our society. Many people who are afflicted have no idea of how to resolve the persistent unhappiness it causes. I discuss this cultural dynamic further in chapter 8.

My empathy training workshops consist of teaching people how to perceive beyond the superficial and how to express what they perceive, as John learned to do. Group experiences provide opportunities to understand how you and others perceive and to become more aware of your biases and preconceived notions that interfere with clear relating. It takes time and discipline to expand your empathic abilities and to know how to choose people in your life who are motivated to do the same.

Through empathic interactions, we have the unique opportunity to rewrite our story. We can discover, once and for all, the truth of who we really are and what in life truly brings love, fulfillment, and balance.

We are born with the capacity for empathy. However, whether that capacity develops depends on how others interact with us. Empathic role models in the early years of our lives can help its development. But if you were not fortunate enough to have empathic parents, or others who understood how to react from an empathic perspective, you can still develop this important skill with the right training. Once you expand your empathic range, you can identify your misguided core beliefs and learn to recognize the cognitive distortions that increase stress and reduce your ability to be close to others.

> It takes time and discipline to expand your empathic abilities and to know how to choose people in your life who are motivated to do the same.

In our fast-paced culture, many people have difficulty learning how to slow down, listen, and interact empathically. However, empathy is unquestionably the most important capacity for a successful personal and professional life. It is critical to maintaining intimacy and healthy working relationships. It allows us to see others accurately and to fall in love with a real person (real love) instead of falling prey to ill-fated attempts to love an illusion that cannot be maintained over time. If we develop our empathic attunement toward others, and expect the same in return, we become part of the solution to a society that is drifting into self-absorption. The health of our culture is dependent on our efforts.

JOURNAL QUESTIONS

- Would those close to you describe you as a driven person?
- If so, how can you begin to lessen your intensity?
- Are you very sensitive to being humiliated?
- What are the reasons you have become so afraid of failure?
- Do you believe that the most likely way to win respect is through achievement?
- When you have felt respected by others for achievement, how long did the good feeling last?
- Can you give examples of how your achievements have won you the genuine respect of others?
- Do you constantly evaluate your performance, and does your mood fluctuate accordingly?
- Do you feel insecure if you are with other people who are better off financially?
- If so, can you describe what they have in life that you cannot attain with your financial status?
- Can you describe the delusions you may have been living with as your core values?
- What realistic perspectives have you gained to help you alter any misguided core values?

TAKE ACTION

If you feel you have lost the joyful part of you through excessive focus on achievement, here's an exercise that may help. List experiences you have had that have given you lasting joy — for example, a vacation with your family or friends. Make an effort to engage others close to you in an activity that is joy-based, not achievement-based. Let the others involved know why you are arranging this activity.

Let them know how you have lost your way in life, and how you want their help in regaining the joyful part of you that has been dormant because of misguided illusions.

CBT STEPS

CBT involves several practical steps:

- Identify triggers like anger, sadness, stress, and anxiety.
- Record the thoughts or beliefs that surface as a result of a particular trigger.
- Record the consequences of this trigger and the thoughts attached to it.

For instance, the trigger may be anxiety about giving a presentation at work; the resultant belief is "I am going to look incompetent"; and the resultant consequence could be insomnia.

The final step is to create a new belief. You must tell yourself, "I have presented this material before" and "I am competent and I will do well." The new consequence is "I was appreciated for my competence and my hard work" or "My preparation brought much respect among my colleagues."

COGNITIVE DISTORTIONS

For each cognitive distortion discussed in this chapter — *catastrophizing*, *mind reading*, and *ignoring the positive* — list the following: activating event (the trigger), belief, consequence (behavioral and emotional), new belief, and new consequence. For example:

Cognitive distortion: Catastrophizing
Activating event: I have been asked to speak at a conference.
Belief: I don't know enough to speak in front of so many people.
Consequence: Anxiety, stress, self-doubt

New belief: I know I have the experience to speak in public successfully.

New consequence: I discussed my fears with one of my trusted colleagues, who helped me prepare. Now I am feeling a little anxious, but overall I am confident that I will perform well.

CHAPTER 6

CBT in Action
Combating the Distortions of Personalization and Blame

What will it profit you if you gain the whole world and lose your soul?

MATTHEW 16:26

Last month, Phil finally left his lucrative corporate sales job to take a position as a consultant to a small startup. Phil had worked for his prestigious company for thirteen years. Following the third re-organization in four years, Phil was assigned to work under an individual who had been labeled "the psychopath" by the sales force. He earned this label because although he is bright and seen as a key player in increasing the profit margin of his company year after year, he is also dishonest. He is noted for humiliating people in front of others, and he has talked condescendingly several times to Phil when he has presented weekly reports at staff meetings. Phil's boss is not well liked or trusted, but in Phil's opinion, these characteristics actually make him more successful at his job than most. "He can close deals with the best of them. People seldom realize that they have just been set up, and they only realize the truth long after the deal pays off. In our senior staff's opinion, he is a success."

When corporations are driven by greed and achievement,

without considering ethics and integrity as important to the work-
force, this dynamic can produce idealization of those who achieve
the most, regardless of character and integrity. Phil became confused
for a time as to what mattered most, and he was not sure whether
integrity and success could exist simultaneously in the corporate
world. The "win at all costs" culture can produce guilt in those who
feel conflicted about this philosophy. The distortion at play is that
you cannot be both honest and ethical and successful.

HUMILIATION AND GUILT: DISTORTED SELF-LOATHING

In 2008, Judith Fisher-Blando wrote a doctoral dissertation titled
"Aggressive Behavior: Workplace Bullying and Its Effect on Job
Satisfaction and Productivity." Her study found that close to 75 percent of employees surveyed had been negatively affected by workplace bullying, whether as victims or bystanders.[1] A 2014 survey by
the Workplace Bullying Institute (WBI) indicates that 65.6 million
U.S. workers were affected by bullying. Bullying was defined as repeated mistreatment; abusive conduct that is threatening, humiliating, or intimidating; work sabotage; or verbal abuse. Of those who
were direct targets of bullying, 61 percent left their jobs. Bosses did
most of the bullying. Only one-third of bullied workers reported
the issue to superiors. Can you imagine the level of stress in these
environments?

The most unfortunate finding from studies of bullying is that
those who are bullied often feel responsible for being under attack.
Another survey by the Workplace Bullying Institute, in 2010, surveyed roughly one thousand people, of whom 98 percent said they
were targets of workplace bullying. In addition:

- 35 percent believed that "somehow I might have deserved the criticisms"
- 28 percent blamed themselves for "not being able to
  counter or confront" the bully

- 22 percent were embarrassed about "allowing it to happen to me"
- only 13 percent felt no shame, saying they "did not invite or deserve the assaults"[2]

Other Workplace Bullying Institute surveys reported the five top reasons individuals felt they were targeted for bullying:

1. refusal to be subservient (being independent)
2. being more technically skilled than the bully
3. being liked by coworkers/customers (being the go-to expert)
4. being ethical and honest
5. not being sufficiently political

From these responses, we can infer that, in essence, it is envy that leads a bully to target those who have admirable strengths. Phil's experience is not uncommon: the tendency toward self-loathing and blame often persists despite the facts. Because empathic CBT is fact-oriented, it can help victims untangle these unfortunate experiences so that people do not hurt themselves after being unjustly hurt by others.

BLAME AND UNDESERVED SHAME

If we have experienced the pain of being bullied, our hurt shapes our self-perception and our outlook, and eventually this pessimism extends to all aspects of our lives. We mistakenly take responsibility for something that is out of our control. Our sense of helplessness is usually accompanied by shame or self-loathing. When directors or managers turn out to be perpetrators of harassment, or when the peers we look to for support and validation turn out to be cruel and sadistic, our world becomes smaller and smaller. Bias and the distorted thinking of

It is envy that leads a bully to target those who have admirable strengths.

overgeneralizing (assuming that what has happened once will continue to happen) then result in a worldview that says other people cannot be trusted. The only way to survive is to steer clear of any unguarded sharing of ourselves.

When Phil was bullied by his manager, for instance, he not only became uncertain whether he had a legitimate complaint, but he also became stressed and agitated. The disparaging remarks his boss had made about him caused insomnia and relentless anxiety. He began to wake at night feeling angry and wanting revenge. When morning came, however, he again felt confused as to whether he or his manager was to blame.

Phil was certainly among the 35 percent who felt responsible for the ill-treatment they received. He was engaging in *personalization*, assuming that he himself was the cause or focus of behavior that in fact had nothing to do with him. He thought the abuse might be caused by his lack of aggressiveness at work. After all, he wasn't really one of the "tough guys" who got the job done. Even though his sales revenue was among the highest in the company, he blamed himself for his lack of "killer instinct." Although he disdained the lack of ethics in the corporate world, he also believed that those who were not concerned with ethics, integrity, and honesty were the most successful and most respected. In the WPI survey, those who valued honesty and high ethics reported being more frequently bullied.

Phil was torn by this ambivalence. His character does not allow deliberate deception, yet he desired the admiration of his manager, who prized success no matter how it was achieved. Despite Phil's impressive performances over several years, he still found himself bullied and demeaned by his superior.

THE LITMUS TEST OF SUCCESS

Phil began his career with an inherent joy and passion for making relationships with diverse groups of people. He particularly enjoyed networking. He liked establishing enduring connections and joint ventures with other companies that led to gain for his company. Over time, he has wrestled with the obsession for success that rules the lives of many in the corporate world today. He came close to sacrificing his soul for a form of success that has yet to make anyone fulfilled and happy for very long. Our soul is the imperceptible aspect of our humanness that contains our true identity. When people and circumstances force us to act in ways that run counter to our natural being, trying to please others in order to stabilize a fragile sense of self, we lose our authenticity. Maintaining our authenticity and integrity is essential to living with minimal stress.

> Our soul is the imperceptible aspect of our humanness that contains our true identity.

We all have a fundamental yearning to be "good enough." If we struggle with our identity and doubt that our essence (our soul) is basically good, we feel compelled to compensate and prove that we are "good enough" every day of our lives.

Phil had lost his way in the corporate arena. He succeeded on his own terms but ultimately became confused by the ethics of his superiors and peers. As I was meeting with a vice president of a local company recently, I thought of Phil's dilemma. This executive praised one of his employees for being obstinate, aggressive, and unwilling to take no for an answer in a meeting with a client. He was thrilled to tell me of closing a major deal. He was impressed with his main "lieutenant." Once again, I was hearing of the norms of a world increasingly devoid of integrity and honesty.

> Maintaining our authenticity and integrity is essential to living with minimal stress.

I am certainly not condemning everyone in the business world. I have helped many successful people negotiate this rocky terrain while maintaining their genuine selves in the process. And no industry is immune to compromised ethics.

Phil's boss was demeaning and insulting, but it still took great courage on Phil's part to walk away from a position that commanded a high salary and bonuses. He interviewed with several other companies before accepting a position with a small company that he was convinced conducted its business with integrity and decency. Today, although he still worries about having reduced his income and status, he is relieved and much happier.

Phil asked me a very important question the other day. "What kept me from completely losing myself? I was really on the edge. The more he demeaned me for not being more aggressive and more ruthless, the more I doubted myself. Then, by the grace of God, I somehow pulled myself out of the gutter and came back to life." Phil wanted to know why some people fall into the abyss of greed and some do not. After all, greed is quite tempting for all of us. Fame, glory, and status will be yours, it promises, if you just work endlessly and rationalize your unethical behavior. All your colleagues are doing the same, so what's the big deal? No one in your work world will disapprove. In fact, you may gain status for winning at all costs and lose status for not being willing to play as hard as possible.

THE HEART'S LONGING FOR AUTHENTICITY

I think the answer to Phil's question about how he was able to turn his back on his lucrative but destructive job was that he could not, in the end, live with an inauthentic self. On the deepest level, our sense of self is governed by what is real and genuine, which is our inborn desire to do and be good. We are inherently virtuous, compassionate, and empathic. These qualities lay dormant in Phil's boss and in many of his colleagues. Our inherent goodness is denied when we have not been treated fairly. When that happens, we either reject the behavior of the perpetrators, or we join the perpetrators' team out of fear and lack of confidence.

Over time, Phil and I developed an empathic bond, which

allowed Phil to feel free to explore his core beliefs and core values. He knew I had worked as a consultant for several local corporations. He asked me who impressed me and who did not. Of course I did not reveal names, but we did discuss our shared distaste for arrogance, greed, and deceit. He began to regain his belief in character and integrity, and he speculated that his boss had become a corporate tyrant most likely because of being exposed to tyranny in his personal life.

> On the deepest level, our sense of self is governed by what is real and genuine, which is our inborn desire to do and be good.

To Phil's credit, he did not fall prey to group-think, a concept developed by the psychologist Irving Janis in 1971.[3] Janis defined *groupthink* as the psychological drive for consensus at any cost, which suppresses disagreement and prevents the appraisal of alternatives in cohesive decision-making groups.

Janis listed eight symptoms of groupthink:

1. Illusion of invulnerability: Excessive optimism that encourages taking extreme risks.
2. Collective rationalization: Members discount warnings and do not question their assumptions.
3. Belief in inherent morality: Members believe in the rightness of their cause and therefore ignore the ethical or moral consequences of their decisions.
4. Stereotyped views of out-groups: Negative views of the "enemy" make tactful, empathic responses to conflict seem unnecessary.
5. Direct pressure on dissenters: Members are under pressure not to express opposition to the group's views.
6. Self-censorship: Doubts and deviations from the perceived group consensus are not expressed.
7. Illusion of unanimity: The majority view and judgments are assumed to be unanimous.

8. Self-appointed "mindguards": Members protect the group and the leader from information that is problematic or contradictory to the group's cohesiveness, view, and/or decisions.

Phil is an independent thinker by nature, and he could not sacrifice his internal moral principles to the groupthink of his boss and peers. After many sleepless nights and intense discussions, he realized he had to move on. A person with a weaker character and less faith in his ability to be simultaneously successful and genuine would probably have been more amenable to his boss's edicts.

Phil's difficulties and ambivalence were prolonged by a negative schema he created, supported by the cognitive distortions of *personalization and blame* and *overgeneralizing.* An empathic connection allowed him to examine the facts of his situation more objectively, and ultimately he was set free by his strong desire to be truthful to himself while maintaining his integrity. Without sharing our feelings and concerns with others, we can lose our way and create negative schemas that we cannot examine clearly or objectively on our own. Giving and receiving empathy sets the stage for clear thinking and is a very important factor in creating and maintaining resilience.

JOURNAL QUESTIONS

- What aspects of Phil's journey do you identify with?
- Would you have had the courage to walk away from the money and status as he did?
- If not, what would prevent you from doing so?
- Do you feel that you are locked in to your present position, with little chance of securing employment elsewhere?

- If so, what are the objective facts that you believe limit your alternatives?
- Are you exposed, like Phil, to pressure to violate ethical norms in your work life?
- If so, how do you cope with such demands? Do you comply? Do you object?
- If you comply, what effect does that decision have on your sense of self?
- Do you find yourself going along with behaviors at work that you know those close to you would disapprove of?
- Of the eight symptoms of groupthink, which are you most vulnerable to in your current situation?
- What strategies have you developed to cope with the pressures of groupthink?

COGNITIVE DISTORTIONS

For both cognitive distortions discussed in this chapter — *personalization and blame* and *overgeneralizing* — list the following: activating event (the trigger), belief, consequence (behavioral and emotional), new belief, and new consequence. For example:

Cognitive distortion: Personalization and blame
Activating event: My boss humiliated me at a staff meeting.
Belief: If I were more competent, he would leave me alone.
Consequence: Self-criticism, shame, embarrassment
New belief: His behavior has nothing to do with my competence.
New consequence: I am not taking responsibility for his sadistic behavior; I will contact HR for guidance.

TAKE ACTION

Discuss the ethical environment in your company or community with someone close to you, and ask that person whether you exhibit any of the symptoms of groupthink. Record your answers in your journal. Be as honest as you can with yourself and your friend.

CHAPTER 7

CBT in Action
Combating Negative Self-Talk and
Ending the Cycle of Stress

There are many wonderful things, but because we have focused on what
is wrong, we have not been able to touch what is right.

THICH NHAT HANH, *A Lifetime of Peace*

We learn how to talk to ourselves based on our early interactions with others. If you were encouraged to experiment, play, color, or throw a ball without your caregivers judging or criticizing you, it is likely that you can try new things with excitement and limited stress. If, however, you were watched closely and criticized often, and especially if one or both of your parents were critical and demanded perfection, you most likely emerged with a punitive inner voice. You probably didn't enjoy trying new things in their presence because you knew very early in life that you were not free to experiment without judgment. The difference between having an understanding inner voice and having a punitive inner voice is dramatic.

Children who grow up surrounded with empathy develop a soothing inner voice. This assures them that even if they cannot hit a home run to win the game, or be voted the most popular person in the class, they are still worthy of love. In contrast, in an environment where empathy is lacking or deficient, a child develops a punitive inner voice that continually repeats the message, "You have not done enough." This often leads to the self-defeating conclusion "You are not enough," or its corollary, "You are not good enough."

Positive thoughts produce neurochemicals that calm you and allow you to focus and perceive clearly. Negative thoughts do the opposite, creating a stress response that limits concentration, memory, and clarity of perception.

People often want to avoid recognizing how negative their inner voice can be. It can be scary to actually slow down and listen to the nature of your thoughts. When you wake in the morning, your first thoughts set the stage for your day. Positive thoughts produce neurochemicals that calm you and allow you to focus and perceive clearly. Negative thoughts do the opposite, creating a stress response that limits concentration, memory, and clarity of perception. By becoming aware of the familiar, previously recorded messages that you play each day, which can provoke the stress response, you can learn to change the recording. You need to hit the pause button instead of playing the whole album and stop the music that drains your energy and limits your potential. It is time to recognize the familiar self-defeating phrases you utter and make the necessary changes to your internal dialogue.

WORRY INVENTORY

- Do you worry about your to-do list as soon as you wake?
- Do you immediately start worrying about all the things you have to do and the awful things that will happen, or the stress you will experience, if you don't get everything done?
- Do you worry about your kids, your spouse, your parents, your boss, and your ability to provide what all these people need?

- To what degree do these kinds of thoughts continue throughout the day?

You probably don't recognize how often you ask these types of questions and project the negative outcomes that you fear into the future. When you have a critical inner voice, you are likely to internalize stress. You blame yourself for situations that are out of your control. You probably have difficulty differentiating when the cause of a particular event is situational and when it is personal. You have already developed negative thoughts about the stress you may encounter before it actually exists, and this internal negativity makes you far more likely to overreact to a stressful situation. It is then not the situation itself that initiates the stress response but your thoughts about stress. If you expect to not be able to manage stress successfully, your bias becomes self-fulfilling.

A client of mine, who is a problem drinker, was living with guilt for secretly drinking unbeknownst to her husband. She would automatically feel guilty and take responsibility for her husband's angry outbursts. These actually had nothing to do with her drinking. She was primed for taking responsibility for his anger, regardless of its root cause. When you have been uttering negative remarks to yourself and triggering the release of stress hormones in the process, you are primed for the cognitive distortion of *ignoring situational and contextual factors*.

Small shifts in the language people use to refer to the self during introspection consequentially influence their ability to regulate their thoughts, feelings, and behavior under social stress, even for vulnerable individuals.

We can use various strategies to silence self-criticism. Studies by the psychologist Ethan Kross of the University of Michigan and his colleagues have shown that "small shifts in the language people refer to the self during introspection consequentially influence their ability to regulate thoughts, feelings, and behavior under social stress, even for vulnerable individuals." Dr. Kross used the example of the NBA star Lebron James's interview when he decided to move from Cleveland to Miami to play. James initially spoke using the pronoun *I*, but when he commented that he didn't want to make an emotional decision, he switched to using his own name: "I wanted to do what's best for Lebron James and to do what makes Lebron James happy." The researchers concluded that referring to himself by name, in the third person, allowed him to distance himself from his emotions to enhance self-regulation.[1] This tendency has been confirmed in additional studies, and it relates to psychological distancing strategies that allow people to feel more in control when they are in stressful situations. Aaron Beck, the founder of cognitive behavioral therapy, believed that distancing allowed individuals to think objectively about irrational thoughts and believed it to be an important part of effective CBT. Distancing is similar to taking an empathic stance, helping us avoid personalizing situations by stepping back and trying to see the forest rather than the trees.

> Distancing is similar to taking an empathic stance, helping us avoid personalizing situations by stepping back and trying to see the forest rather than the trees.

CONSTRUCTIVE SELF-TALK

Tom is a warmhearted, middle-aged man. He and his wife are very committed family people, with close ties to their extended family. Tom has a very critical internal voice and often feels guilty saying no to people who want something from him, even though he feels a great deal of stress as a result. Tom told me of his cousin, who had just called to say how excited his family was to spend a week at Tom's Cape Cod house in the first week of July. He told me, "Doc, we never invited them this year. We did last year, and they came supposedly for the weekend, but ended up staying six days. They came with nothing, did not even offer to buy food, nothing! They are very particular. His wife only eats organic food. He likes certain kinds of wine. They drove us crazy! I feel guilty telling them we don't really want them to be with us for a week."

Tom finds himself in these kinds of situations frequently, as he finds it hard to set limits with people. He ruminates constantly about what to do and how to let people know what he really wants. The Cape Cod issue is an example of his punitive internal voice telling him that he is being selfish, that he "should" just extend himself to offer hospitality to his relatives and share the house he has the good fortune to own. He tries to suppress this voice by staying up late watching TV, eating all the wrong foods, and having a few beers. He then wakes up the next morning even more critical of himself than the day before. He tries to use self-affirming internal statements to ease his stress, but these efforts only provide temporary relief.

A review of two dozen studies published in the journal *Perspectives on Psychological Science* found that encouraging messages like "You will be successful" or "You have the confidence to succeed" are not always the most successful kinds of self-talk.[2] The researchers call their new method *instructional self-talk*. They describe it as a series of statements that provide a planned sequence of behaviors that will lead to a successful conclusion.

For instance, Tom could construct the following internal plan: "First I will call my cousin and tell him I need a few minutes of his time. Then I will tell him that it is difficult for me to say, but we have decided to spend more time alone this summer and not have as much company as in the past. I will let him know that we would love to go out for dinner or go to the beach with him and his wife. I will also add that I hope he understands that I only have a few weeks of vacation and that my wife and I both need some quiet down time." After Tom and I discussed this approach, he addressed his cousin successfully.

Tom needed an opportunity to talk about his fear of disappointing people. His mother was very sensitive and often hurt when he and his wife did not visit her on weekends, or when he did not call her every other day. The guilt he then felt was significant and stress producing. Guilt often signifies a childhood during which a child was taught to be responsible for an adult's well-being.

An empathic interchange allowed Tom to return to the scene of the crime. Once he realized the origin of his punitive, guilty self-talk, he could begin to restructure the way he talks to himself, based on realistic expectations, without taking on responsibility for other people's reactions.

Guilt often signifies a childhood during which a child was taught to be responsible for an adult's well-being.

Tom, a project manager for a large consulting company, also felt encouraged by the research that I shared with him from the psychologist Steven Rogelberg, of the University of North Carolina at Chapel Hill. The goal of Dr. Rogelberg and his team was to compare the kinds of self-talk employed by effective and ineffective managers. They had subjects write letters to themselves about their accomplishments and plans for the future.[3] The constructive self-talkers wrote encouraging and positive accounts, while the negative self-talkers wrote in a gloomy style that accented negative outcomes. The research team found that constructive self-talkers, as expected, scored higher in the categories of leadership, creativity, originality, and accurate perceptions of job stress.

Tom saw the value of changing his punitive internal voice to an understanding voice in both personal and professional settings. He realized that his previous way of thinking was depleting his brain chemistry and compromising his well-being. A more realistic voice would support his entire physiology.

STEPS TO CHANGE SELF-TALK

In order to change your self-talk from negative to positive, you first need to uncover the origin of your negative story. Use your empathy to understand how you came to repeat certain phrases to yourself. This will help you to stop blaming yourself, as you realize that you have internalized a view of how you thought others perceived you.

1. Write in your journal the familiar records you play in your mind that support negative self-talk. For instance, "I'm not pretty enough," "I sound so stupid when I speak," "I'm too flabby," or "I'm not successful." Commit to hitting the pause button every day as soon as you hear yourself utter these phrases.

2. Replace these phrases with the truth. Practice every day repeating what you have heard about yourself from people you trust. Gain some distance and try to be as objective as possible. Imagine you are one of your good friends. For instance, you might tell yourself, "I may not be stunning, but I am attractive," "I may mispronounce a few words on occasion, but generally I speak well," "I may be a little overweight, but I am working on my fitness and I am improving weekly," or "I am not independently wealthy, but I have had a successful career and have helped many people."

3. Practice differentiating situational causes from personal causes in problematic situations. You will be far less likely to activate your critical self-talk if you can use your empathy to see clearly who or what is responsible for various circumstances. For instance, suppose your wife comes home from visiting her moody sister. Rather than giving you a kiss as she usually does when she enters the house, she makes an exasperated sound before speaking to you. Instead of personalizing the situation and assuming you have done something wrong, ask her what's bothering her so that you get the facts, not some distorted theory you create that fuels negativity.

You were not born with a negative internal voice: it was learned, and it can definitely be unlearned. If you keep practicing the recommended steps, you will likely find yourself being kinder to yourself.

JOURNAL QUESTIONS

- How do you think you came to develop a negative internal voice?
- Whom did you interact with who had a significant influence on your internal dialogue?
- Can you write empathically about how you understand this person's motivation to influence you?
- What steps are you taking daily to keep your internal voice positive?

COGNITIVE DISTORTIONS

For both cognitive distortions discussed in this chapter — *self-criticism to motivate yourself* and *ignoring situational and contextual factors* — list the following: activating event (the trigger), belief, consequence (behavioral and emotional), new belief, and new consequence. For example:

Cognitive distortion: Ignoring situational factors
Activating event: I am not getting any response from potential employers despite sending out many résumés.
Belief: People are not impressed with my qualifications.
Consequence: Self-doubt, withdrawal, passivity
New belief: The job market is tight for everyone; I have faith that I will find employment eventually.
New consequence: Rather than sulking and withdrawing, I will continue to be proactive, and when the economy picks up, I will be employed.

TAKE ACTION

Tell a friend or relative how you are trying to change the way you talk to yourself. Ask them to give you periodic feedback on the differences they see in your behavior as a result. Record the feedback in your journal. Continue this exercise for several weeks. Make a chart like the one below, and list your negative self-talk and your corrected positive thinking. For instance:

NEGATIVE SELF-TALK	POSITIVE THINKING
I've never been comfortable at new social gatherings.	It's a chance to change an old record.
It's too hard.	I'll ask for help and find out.
I never get the help I need.	I'll ask for what I need; I won't wait for others to read my mind.
I'm lazy and not very bright.	I'm uninformed, not unintelligent.
There's no way I can complete that course.	If I make the effort, I will likely be fine.
I can't imagine being calm.	I can imagine anything I want.
No one cares about me.	I'll reach out and see who responds.
I can't go to a gym; I'm not athletic.	I don't have to be an athlete to work out.

SELF-TALK SURVEY

- How often do you criticize your intelligence?
  ❑ Hourly ❑ Daily ❑ Weekly ❑ Infrequently ❑ Never
- How often do you criticize your appearance?
  ❑ Hourly ❑ Daily ❑ Weekly ❑ Infrequently ❑ Never
- How often do you predict negative outcomes?
  ❑ Hourly ❑ Daily ❑ Weekly ❑ Infrequently ❑ Never
- How often do you hear yourself saying that people don't like you?
  ❑ Hourly ❑ Daily ❑ Weekly ❑ Infrequently ❑ Never

- How often do you repeat to yourself some of the negative phrases you heard about yourself as a child?
  ❑ Hourly ❑ Daily ❑ Weekly ❑ Infrequently ❑ Never
- How often do you call yourself a loser, failure, fraud, or dummy?
  ❑ Hourly ❑ Daily ❑ Weekly ❑ Infrequently ❑ Never
- How often do you find yourself wishing you had the material possessions of someone you know?
  ❑ Hourly ❑ Daily ❑ Weekly ❑ Infrequently ❑ Never
- When you look in the mirror, how often do you say something negative about yourself?
  ❑ Hourly ❑ Daily ❑ Weekly ❑ Infrequently ❑ Never
- How often do you say to yourself that your physique is disgusting, unattractive, or ugly?
  ❑ Hourly ❑ Daily ❑ Weekly ❑ Infrequently ❑ Never
- How often do you say to yourself that you hate yourself?
  ❑ Hourly ❑ Daily ❑ Weekly ❑ Infrequently ❑ Never

Scoring

Score 4 points for every "hourly" response, 3 for "daily," 2 for "weekly," 1 for "infrequently," and 0 for never. Calculate your total score.

16 or more points: significant self-abuse
12–15 points: moderate self-abuse
7–11 points: mild self-abuse
0–6 points: positive self-talk

CHAPTER 8

CBT in Action
Combating Performance Addiction

> My ruthless desire to win at all costs served me well on the bike,
> but the level it went to, for whatever reason, is a flaw.
> That desire, that attitude, that arrogance.
>
> LANCE ARMSTRONG, interview with Oprah Winfrey, January 18, 2013

D o you wake up in the morning with a feeling of dread in your heart? Do you have a sense that the day is going to be difficult? Do you question whether you will have the energy to get through it while functioning at the level you desire? Do you immediately start thinking of the to-do list in your mind, the one you went to bed with and now must complete if you're not going to feel even more stressed? If so, you may be one of many people suffering from a form of *performance addiction.*

Performance addiction is the belief that perfecting your appearance and increasing your social or professional status will bring you love and respect. It is an irrational belief system created by early experiences and reinforced by our current culture. Most people realize, when prompted to question the validity of this core belief, that it is a cognitive distortion. Nevertheless, they cannot stop themselves from living according to the dictates of perfectionism. It's as if they believe that they can perfect their way to happiness.

The sports psychologist Andrew Hill, of York St. John University in England, analyzed findings from forty-three studies examining the relationship between burnout, stress, and perfectionism. Perfectionism that was manifested as working toward goals in a proactive style was not particularly harmful, but when perfectionists were overly worried about mistakes, disappointing others, or measuring up to impossible standards, it led to depression, anxiety, fatigue, eating disorders, and earlier mortality.

Performance addiction is the belief that perfecting your appearance and increasing your social or professional status will bring you love and respect.

What makes us vulnerable to the stress of perfectionism? What actually provides the love and respect we all crave? This chapter shows how performance addiction creates inordinate stress and takes its toll on relationships and family. This behavior often makes a person so focused on individual pursuits that there is a lack of regard — essentially a lack of empathy — for the needs of those who matter most.

Performance addicts are known for sacrificing intimacy for achievement. They are so preoccupied and stressed that they have great difficulty being emotionally available for closeness with others.

We can reduce stress and increase our self-worth when we know how to maintain intimacy. When we leave home with love in our hearts, we are more resilient and able to deal with the stressors of the day.

THE SCENE OF THE CRIME

What I call the "scene of the crime" is the time when you established the core belief that you could gain love and respect by performing well. If you grew up in a home where you received validation mainly through achievement, or had parents who were perfectionists themselves, you likely adopted this misguided way of looking at yourself and the world.

Very early in life, we learn which of our behaviors gain attention and affection. We begin to form our view of success. We develop ideas about how to reach a level of competence that will provide us with self-worth. Because these ideas develop so early, the cognitive distortions associated with them can be very difficult to alter. I know from many years of clinical practice that CBT alone is often not sufficient. We need to go back to the scene of the crime.

Early in life we create a story about ourselves based on what we think is being reflected back to us by the significant people in our lives. If the important people in our lives regard achievement and perfection as the keys to love and esteem, we adopt the same distorted feelings. We may learn to compete and excel in a very narrow area of life. Overachieving can bring us superficial applause for how much we accomplish or for the level of success we achieve, while our personal life can suffer and we accumulate inordinate levels of stress. We may think we are being loved for our efforts, but our deeper needs are still unmet, because these efforts do not bring us lasting love and respect. We have to keep trying harder and harder to attain the approval we long for.

Most people with performance addiction know something is missing, but they have no idea of how to satisfy their longings. When good performance doesn't bring happiness, they think they must perform even better. They end up trying to work harder, faster, and more proficiently to fill the void. Performance addicts believe they can perfect their way to happiness. More and more effort with the same dysfunctional belief system produces the same negative outcome. This is the nature of an addiction.

Trying to resolve childhood hurts by high achievement or perfecting our appearance creates anxiety. The resultant cortisol allows the brain to be rewired by stress. Cortisol limits clear thinking and compromises the ability to see and perceive accurately.

GENDER DIFFERENCES

Performance addicts usually have résumés that read well, but they seem to have a low opinion of their own professional achievements or personal appearance. They are what I call "scoreboard watchers," always taking inventory of how well or how poorly they are performing or how great or dismal they look. Men who are performance addicts seem preoccupied with money, status, and image. Women tend to be self-conscious about their appearance, believing that good looks are the path to happiness. These are not, of course, rigid distinctions: women, too, often feel highly driven to succeed professionally, and men can be overly preoccupied with their appearance and weight. Ultimately, only learning what truly brings us love and respect can set us free from the stress that performance addiction creates.

DISTORTED VIEW OF VULNERABILITY

A few years ago, I met David, a former professional athlete who had suffered in silence with stress, anxiety, and feelings of humiliation. David had been a star high school and college athlete. He was destined for the pro leagues, but as time went on, he enjoyed playing less and less. He wanted to be free of the constant pressure and the monitoring by coaches, trainers, publicists, and agents, and the intrusions of fans. David is quite handsome, tall, with lean muscle structure and a wide grin that says, "I'm happy and enjoying life."

Although he reached the professional level in his sport, he was plagued by anxiety and insomnia during his competitive career. As a result, he never lived up to the potential his coaches and fans believed he had. David was given one of my previous books, *Performance Addiction*. After reading the book several times, and at the insistence of his wife, he finally called me. He felt enormously ashamed to be in my office. "If any of the guys in my world knew I was here, they wouldn't believe it. It's a little better since all the publicity about stressed athletes, but I still wonder how my friends would feel. We live the 'buck up' theory of life. I am sure you are aware of the 'do it yourself' mentality."

Interestingly, David noticed a book on my shelf, *American Master Spy*, a World War II description of the activities of the Office of Strategic Services (OSS), a forerunner of the CIA. David told me he was a World War II buff. "I read everything I can get my hands on. Can you tell me a bit about this book? I have read several about the OSS." My father appears in this book, photographed in Algiers with a secret mission team. David was instantly interested in my father, espionage, and how agents "could have the courage to persist with death facing them at all times."

I told David I learned a great deal from the way my father talked about the war. He refused to talk about the details of his thirteen parachute jumps in enemy territory until the later years of his life. As I spoke of my dad, David looked surprised, and at the same time, I could see relief on his face. David's father, an ex-marine, was extremely demanding and critical of his son. David has no memory of his father ever acknowledging any weakness or shortcoming, although he drank excessively. He expressed his poor opinion of David through angry outbursts. David's father's anger became his own anger over time. He felt unable to defend his mother and himself, and as a result he grew to hate vulnerability, as it reminded him of the awful feelings he had as a child. The stressful environment of his home made him want to block out any feelings of helplessness.

When we are excessively vulnerable early in life, we develop an intolerance for feeling out of control. We come to believe that being vulnerable is an unnatural state of mind that can only bring pain and suffering. As David reached adulthood trying to eliminate any chance of reexperiencing childhood hurts, he unfortunately chose a profession that supported the denial of any emotions except anger.

In the culture of his sport, anger was seen as motivating a person to compete more intensely. David had to learn that his anger was hiding his fears and not allowing him to cope constructively.

Any distortion of the truth places us in a compromised position. We cannot come to terms with who we are if we are conducting our lives on false premises. David came to realize that he struggled with anger, like his father, and he discovered through our conversations that his anger was a means of letting adrenaline flow to create a superficial sense of control. He did not understand that we all feel vulnerable at times. In the face of certain challenges, vulnerability can be an asset if we acknowledge that all humans are periodically helpless. Feeling vulnerable can help us know when to let go and give in to the situation. It can allow us to reduce rather than deny stress.

> When we are excessively vulnerable early in life, we develop an intolerance for feeling out of control. We come to believe that being vulnerable is an unnatural state of mind that can only bring pain and suffering.

At one point, I told David that I thought there was a parallel between my father's wartime experience and his experience. I said that many athletes do not see the strength of vulnerability, and this prevents them from getting the support they need. He acknowledged that this is true. "But I always thought it's better to plan for the worst, no surprises, just don't let anyone know you're thinking negative."

I explained that there is a difference between being negative and being realistic. We discussed the cognitive distortions of *ignoring the positive* and *black-and-white thinking*. People who acknowledge the positive aspects of their lives live longer; they have reduced rates of death from cardiovascular disease, stronger immune systems, and a greater sense of overall well-being. Black-and-white thinking tends to fuel the idea that we can predict outcomes, with a bias toward a negative outcome.

Living in Massachusetts, David is quite familiar with the New

England Patriots football team and in fact has long-time friends in the organization. The Patriots, at the time of our last session, were preparing for a Super Bowl matchup against the Seattle Seahawks (a fiercely competitive team led by a legendary defense and an explosive offense). I asked David if the Patriots coach, Bill Belichek, would be preparing for all aspects of the game, taking into consideration the strengths and weaknesses of his team's opponent. "Of course! You know that Bill will be highlighting every possible scenario. The guy is amazing in that he seems to be able to anticipate every possibility." I pointed out that Belichek has this ability partly because he is aware of the vulnerabilities of his team. Knowing its weak points, he can prepare with all factors in mind, akin to a general who is not arrogant but realistic before he plans a strategy for a battle.

> People who acknowledge the positive aspects of their lives live longer; they have reduced rates of death from cardiovascular disease, stronger immune systems, and a greater sense of overall well-being.

FEAR DISTORTS REALITY

David has learned to deny certain realities out of a fear of failure: he plans for the worst, thinking that this outlook will allow him to be prepared for dismal outcomes. He is afraid that acknowledging his emotions and concerns will lead to negativity and poor performance. This way of thinking puts him at a decided disadvantage. A true optimist, a person who can think positively but realistically, can take in all relevant aspects of a situation; the key to having a wide lens of awareness is to not become emotionally limited by excessive worry or concerns.

THE HUMBLE, HONEST RISK TAKER

David has now participated in several of my empathic CBT workshops. Through them, he has made contact with men and women who have not only been successful athletes but are also successful in their personal and professional lives. David was initially surprised that such competent people would attend my workshops and acknowledge their vulnerabilities. He was surprised that they could be honest about stressors and anxieties and still perform at a high level. He has been working with the embedded belief that in order to be successful, you have to deny any potential negative outcome and move forward without hesitation. Fear of the truth makes us anxious and afraid. We seek relief through alcohol or other dysfunctional patterns. Understanding and addressing the truth makes us wiser, humbler, and ultimately more honest people.

When we embrace honesty and humility, we are actually more able to take risks, because we are prepared for all possibilities. Instead of fixating on success as the only permissible outcome, we come to accept that sometimes life will go well, and sometimes it will not. In the end, we believe that success will likely come our way if we are prepared. We have the courage to occasionally take the plunge and have an opportunity to discover what we can do, and who we can become.

> Fear of the truth makes us anxious and afraid. We seek relief through alcohol or other dysfunctional patterns. Understanding and addressing the truth makes us wiser, humbler, and ultimately more honest people.

As David participated more in group discussions, he slowly developed more faith in himself. He learned to lessen the demands of the internal voice that for many years has insisted on perfection. Interestingly, as David has quieted his punitive self-talk, he has become more involved in the group discussions and offered many worthwhile insights into group members' behaviors that he had previously missed or misinterpreted.

By listening to group members acknowledging their imperfections, David has been able to shed the burden of perfection. Witnessing good, gifted individuals struggling with the same anxieties and stresses he has encountered, he has seen that they have learned to participate fully in life without obsessively seeking perfection. Most important, he has learned that as people open themselves up to the world and to themselves, they free themselves from the tyranny of living up to an unrealistic self-image. These individuals have become themselves. They take risks because they don't take themselves too seriously. They have room to experiment, to learn, to fail, and ultimately to win. There is nothing that produces greater creativity and high achievement in life than being comfortable in your own skin, accepting who you are and who you aren't. If you are suffering from performance addiction, please realize that this perspective can be changed so that you can achieve without the intense fear of failure.

> There is nothing that produces greater creativity and high achievement in life than being comfortable in your own skin, accepting who you are and who you aren't.

I have always marveled at those with average ability who become good athletes. They succeed in part because they don't have the burden of constantly comparing themselves to the great ones. They are often more likely to actualize their potential than those who are more naturally gifted because they are accepting of and accustomed to hard work and the benefits it provides to their sense of self.

OBSESSED-WITH-SUCCESS COMPLEX

Many in our culture are afflicted with *performance addiction*. When we value high achievement above all, we are often surprised to discover that some of the most successful people in a given field are not particularly balanced and may actually have a fragile sense of self. We sometimes learn that these people ultimately turn to drugs, sexual addictions, and impulsive behavior. It seems impossible that such high achievers can be so troubled internally. We have bought into the common belief that high achievement and performance in one arena will make everything else fall into place.

The fallacy of this belief is evident in the personal lives of some very high achievers. I have worked with elite athletes and other noted professionals who know very little about how to establish and maintain an intimate relationship. Success in one field does not mean a person has the interpersonal abilities necessary for personal success. High achievers often choose love partners who idealize them for their fame and status rather than for who they are.

True happiness, love, and respect come when people have developed high-level relationship skills, especially the capacity for empathy. Performance addicts tend to rate status over character, achievement over relationships. Ironically, they recover only when they learn, in their hearts and in their heads, that developing relationships is the key to finding what they have been missing for most of their lives. Numerous studies have shown that interpersonal skills are essential to success in the corporate world. Most recently, studies have indicated that empathy is crucial for success in police work, government, education, and politics.

Successful executives have the ability to sense other people's needs and to make them feel heard. Essentially, they have developed the capacity for empathy, or what the psychologist William Ickes called "everyday mind reading."[1]

This same skill set is what performance addicts need to move past image love to real love. Performance addicts have difficulty loving: they base their own lovability on their daily performance. Unfortunately, they expect the same of their partners. They are constantly comparing and contrasting themselves and their partners to others. This tendency drives their perfectionism and creates a stress for all involved. They find it easy to fall in love but difficult to actually love a real person after the binding and blinding effects of early sexual attraction wear off. True love and true sexual intimacy are based on uncritical affection. This type of affection is something the performance addict has never received and does not know how to give.

GOING FORWARD

If you recognize the signs of performance addiction in yourself, you must work hard to develop the interpersonal abilities you need to acquire and foster lasting love — a love based on who we are, not just on what we do or how we look. In the remaining chapters, I highlight the skills you need to reduce stress and develop the resilience for personal and professional success.

Performance addicts have difficulty loving: they base their own lovability on their daily performance.

Since opening his heart and mind, David has not only become closer to friends and fellow group members, but he has reestablished a loving relationship with his wife. They had maintained a distance for years and had little idea of how to regain the love they once had and had expressed so easily. David, with his mistaken beliefs about what true success entails, was seldom present in their relationship. As a result, his wife, Paula, felt alone and on the sidelines of his life. David didn't realize that his quest for stardom was really a search for intimacy. Only recently has he discovered the true way to establish love and respect.

We are meant to love and connect. When this connection happens and endures, it allows us to go out into the world and achieve for the right reasons. Our potential is unleashed through the support of those who truly know us and value our character. This frees us to pursue success without the obsessive fear of failure. If we don't meet a particular goal, we will still have love, because it's not based solely on what we do. This is truly a liberating experience!

JOURNAL QUESTIONS

- How has the stress of performance influenced your life?
- How could you alter your tendency to be overly stressed about performance? Be specific.

- How do you feel when you acknowledge feeling vul-
  nerable?
- Has exposing your vulnerabilities been problematic
  for you?
- Has doing so caused you embarrassment?
- Do you tend to idealize those in power and those with
  status?
- If so, how did you learn to think of them as superior
  to you?
- What aspects of David's life do you identify with?
- Do you understand how the obsession for success can
  interfere with loving relationships?
- How do you allow your work or your quest for success
  to interfere with the relationships in your life? Be very
  specific.
- How will you correct these tendencies?
- What is your plan for learning to place character and
  relationships above image and status?

TAKE ACTION

If performance addiction has prevented you from being fully present to the people closest to you, apologize and make a commitment
to do better in the future. Record your plan and your progress in
your journal, and revisit it weekly.

COGNITIVE DISTORTIONS

For the cognitive distortions discussed in this chapter — *ignoring the positive, holding unrelenting standards*, and *black-and-white
thinking* — list the following: activating event (the trigger), belief,
consequence (behavioral and emotional), new belief, and new consequence. For example:

Cognitive distortion: Unrelenting standards
Activating event: My supervisor noticed an error I made in my report.
Belief: He doesn't think much of me.
Consequence: Self-blame, stress, avoidance of authorities
New belief: One comment from my boss does not mean that he considers me a failure.
New consequence: I can ask him for help when I make mistakes, rather than avoiding him and sulking unnecessarily.

PERFORMANCE ADDICTION QUESTIONNAIRE

Please complete the Performance Addiction Questionnaire in the appendix (page 178). Complete it again at the conclusion of the book, and compare your scores.

CHAPTER 9

Clear Eyes
Perceiving the Truth through Empathy, Not Prejudice

> Perhaps travel cannot prevent bigotry, but by demonstrating that all
> peoples cry, laugh, eat, worry, and die, it can introduce the idea that if we
> try and understand each other, we may even become friends.
>
> MAYA ANGELOU, *Wouldn't Take Nothing for My Journey Now*

I have always been deeply affected by prejudice. I have been called guinea and wop, asked if my family was in the Mafia, told that people like me should not go to college, and asked to not associate with certain friends because I was not of their religious background. However, the prejudice I have endured has been mild compared to the pain of those who suffer daily from distorted views about themselves.

As a result of years spent trying to teach people to rewrite their prejudicial stories about themselves and others, I am keenly aware of how prejudice can spread. It can develop into embedded beliefs and cause inordinate amounts of stress. These inaccurate beliefs hamper a person's potential by creating self-hatred and destroying their spirit. Prejudice reduces trust, creates insecurity, and causes stress between individuals, communities, and nations. Whenever our perceptions are distorted, stress is a likely by-product.

I see patients on the hour five days a week. As we develop a trusting, caring relationship, people often feel free to speak spontaneously, with less inhibition than they express socially. I am continually fascinated and dismayed by the amount of stress that prejudicial thinking and behaving creates.

Along with my own personal experiences, here are a few comments I've heard recently in my practice from people from all walks of life.

"Dogs don't like black people; must be something about their smell."

"We should bomb all the Arabs, starting with Iran."

"I'm not prejudiced, but I feel uncomfortable when my kids get close to Christians."

"I'm not biased, but you know how Jews are. You're not Jewish, are you?"

"My sister is in love with a German she met while traveling. My father won't permit him to enter our house — he can't forget the war."

"Hispanics are taking over this country. All the liberals are telling our kids they need to learn Spanish."

"You can't trust a Palestinian; they are all killers."

"Men lack the empathy gene."

"I love my wife, but if women were leading the world, you know the economy would tank."

"I know intellectually that I am wrong, but I just can't believe a fat person can be that smart."

Each of these statements expresses an untrue bias. When they were made, I could see visible signs of stress on each person's face. Most people are unaware of the level of stress that such untruths create. If you're prejudiced, you are likely afraid. The tension that prejudice causes is often seen as necessary for safety and security. Whether you have biases toward yourself or toward others, you will live with unnecessary stress. Empathy is the tool that enables us to subject these views to rational examination before they are embedded and acted on, consciously or unconsciously.

OPENING A CLOSED DOOR

Would you have the courage to challenge a colleague, friend, or family member who made any of the statements above? Most people say they would, but experience tells me this is hardly ever the case. Most individuals want to avoid conflict and feelings of discomfort, so they change the subject or just remain quiet. Among the greatest abilities any human being can possess are the abilities to tolerate and learn from differences and to address conflict directly, truthfully, and tactfully. These are among the benefits of knowing how to communicate with empathy, which teaches us how to relate with honesty and sensitivity and lessens the likelihood of a defensive reaction. How many people do you know with these skills? If you were willing to learn these skills and teach them to your children, you would unquestionably diminish the stress and tension in our world today.

> Among the greatest abilities any human being can possess are the abilities to tolerate and learn from differences and to address conflict directly, truthfully, and tactfully.

Prejudice toward oneself or others is often the result of a lack of awareness combined with a fragile sense of self. This tendency may be taught and reinforced by the milieu we live in. We mirror the behaviors we see, and our empathy grows or contracts in response to our early encounters. For example, if as a child you spoke and were ignored, if you wanted to tell your parents about your day but they were too preoccupied to understand, or if, when you were hurt, you were told to control your tears, you probably began to avoid expressing enthusiasm or pain, and you would tend to observe your parents and other authority figures to learn what behaviors they deemed acceptable. Children long for approval, and when it is not forthcoming, they seek any means to shore up their self-worth.

If a parent is prejudiced toward an ethnic group or a particular religion, a child learns to feel and think the same way. The child may not suffer low self-esteem but will likely be influenced by distorted perceptions. Over time, this closed way of thinking limits possibilities and friendships with a diverse group of people, ultimately leading to insecurity or anger in the presence of people who are targets of the prejudice.

Sixty-one percent of Americans currently believe that race relations in this country are poor. The percentages have been rising monthly, causing stress and pessimism among blacks and whites alike.[1]

In addition, our world is currently rocked by terrorism and the hatred that leads human beings to believe that they exemplify the right and only way to live and that they must convert others to the same way of life by force, if necessary. It isn't just extremists in poor nations who are guilty of this way of thinking; it is people in our daily lives who think and perceive in the same general way, even if they do not resort to physical violence.

Research at the University of Queensland tested a previous finding that people have much stronger empathy toward those of their own race or ethnic background. The study, conducted by Dr. Ross Cunningham, involved Chinese students new to Australia. The students were shown videos of Chinese and Caucasian actors receiving a painful or nonpainful touch to their cheek and questioned as to the level of empathy they felt for the actors. Those students who indicated that they had more contact with students of other races showed higher levels of empathy than did those students who had contact only with other students like themselves. The students with higher empathy had more daily exposure to those from different backgrounds — not necessarily close relationships, but simply more contact. In essence, familiarity had a significant impact on empathy, regardless of race or ethnic background. Empathy increases and stress decreases with exposure to other groups of people.[2]

When we offer our concern and compassion only to those in our own family, neighborhood, religion, or country, it is often because of our lack of exposure to others. Empathy is born out of a humble love, one that cares for all people, knowing that we are all more alike than dissimilar.

OPENNESS IN TRAGEDY

I recently asked Michael, a young marine who had completed two tours in Iraq, how he found the people in that nation. "I found the people to be warm and welcoming," he said. They really wanted us to be there. However, the local politicians and those in power seemed deceitful and greedy."

This young man saw killing firsthand, witnessing both Iraqi and American lives lost, yet he emerged with an open mind. I asked him how he developed such an attitude. He replied, "My parents taught us to respect everyone who respects us, a simple philosophy with no exceptions."

Michael told me a story about looking for bomb makers in a small village in Iraq. As he kicked open the door of a house, he saw a young sniper sitting on a landing directly above the door, with an automatic weapon aimed at him. He gasped and heard a shot from behind him. The young man fell down the stairs. He looked over his shoulder and realized that a fellow marine had just saved his life by shooting the sniper. Michael then looked at the face of the young man who had just been killed and began to weep. "He looked like me, dark-skinned, tall, wavy black hair; it struck me so powerfully that it could have been me. And did he deserve to die any more than I deserved to live? We were both fighting for what we believe to be true — who knows what actually is. I just felt like I didn't know anything anymore."

Michael's experience displays how an open-minded, empathic individual functioned in ambiguous and unknown territory. He did not fall into the trap of assuming or generalizing about Iraqi people; he found commonality between human beings of different cultures despite the horrific conditions he was exposed to. His choices are a testimony to his ability to think clearly and not allow his emotions to dictate his perceptions. Because Michael is not stressed by inter-actions with people from different backgrounds, he is able to find common ground and common humanity.

Studies by Arne Roets and Alain Van Hiel of Ghent University in Belgium indicate that prejudice and the distorted thinking it pro-duces are more common in people with a low tolerance for ambiguity and uncertainty. They are prone to making quick and firm decisions, and then they generalize based on the most obvious information. They tend to rigidly follow authority and social norms, which give them rules to cling to whenever they feel uncertain or insecure.[3] They suffer from *cognitive conformity:* consciously or unconsciously adapting the views of people with whom we are associated.

The following are other cognitive distortions that are common to biased perceiving and tension:

- Using feelings as the basis of a judgment when the ob-jective evidence does not support your feelings
- Cognitive labeling: mentally labeling a person and not being open to objective evidence to the contrary
- Blaming others
- Failure to consider alternative explanations
- In-group bias: valuing those you consider to be like you more than those unlike you
- Subconscious or unconscious (implicit) biased attitudes

Michael, as we have seen, does not exhibit these qualities or behaviors. He is an unusual and compassionate human being. He didn't hate the person who was trying to kill him. He saw beyond the surface and realized that both he and his potential attacker were proceeding according to their beliefs. In that regard, they not only looked alike, but they also thought alike. Empathy allows us to see beyond and within. Empathy allows us to think through a situation for ourselves rather than relying on superficial judgments.

TRUTH SEEKING

To rid ourselves of the stress caused by prejudice, we must be guided by truth. Empathy is our guide, as it is always based on objective accuracy.

Empathy is part of our genetic endowment. It is akin to a muscle: when it is used, it expands and develops, and when it lies dormant, it atrophies. As we practice empathy, we strengthen our innate ability. It allows us to see beyond the surface, to touch the soul within. Without empathy, we cannot understand who other people are or what their behavior means. Just think of the statement from one of my clients: "Dogs don't like black people; must be something about their smell." Ironically, this statement was made by a very intelligent human being who had himself been the object of a great deal of prejudice. We have a very good relationship, so I feel free to talk to him bluntly. I addressed this prejudice literally by telling him that I have a favorite uncle who is African American and a dog lover. He is an affable, lovable man whom both dogs and humans take to instantly.

My patient said he felt foolish: he had accepted this belief because his dogs never seemed comfortable with the black people on his street when he was growing up. He employed the cognitive distortion of *overgeneralization:* assuming that what happened on one occasion will be true on all occasions. He also didn't consider that the dogs on the street might have been picking up the defensive anxieties of their owners when in the presence of African Americans. "Guess I did what I criticize other people for — jumped to a conclusion based on a very small sample size." I believe he truly meant no ill intent toward blacks, but his early experience and his lack of contact with African Americans allowed his early view to solidify. With an open mind, he corrected his prejudice.

We all reach adulthood with prejudices of some sort. Our responsibility to our world and ourselves is to reexamine the stories we wrote that were based on incorrect information about others and ourselves. People often ask me how anyone could become a terrorist. I reply that if you have been abused, if you are emotionally and financially impoverished, then you are vulnerable to whatever you hear, especially if you long to belong. If you have not been taught to use empathy to examine the accuracy of what you hear, you absorb rather than evaluate. Some people in the world who hate Americans have never met an American. And some Americans think in similar ways. The patient who expressed the racist views above is not generally prejudiced, and he is never going to kill anyone, but if he had grown up emotionally and financially disadvantaged, he might have been vulnerable to recruitment by white supremacists.

> We all reach adulthood with prejudices of some sort. Our responsibility to our world and ourselves is to reexamine the stories we wrote that were based on incorrect information about others and ourselves.

LOVE IS BLIND

We develop certain core beliefs early in life based on the situations we are exposed to and how our parents and significant people in our lives perceive the world and us. These perceptions include gender roles. Some of our distorted learning is innocuous, but some of it can cause serious stress in our relationships.

One of my clients, Rebecca, is quite bright, unusually kind, and very attractive, yet she suffers from a highly stressful life. She enjoyed college, where she did not date much but had good friends, got good grades, and seemed headed for a great career in the business world. Shortly after graduation, she met Ryan. He seemed affable and was already making considerable money, as he had been in the corporate world for five years. They dated. He particularly wanted a partner of the same religion and culture, as she did. She later realized this requirement affected her judgment and was one of the reasons, along with her poor self-concept, that she did not see him clearly. Rebecca, who was vulnerable to negative self-talk like "I'll never find anyone good to love me" and "He's too handsome to want me," was strongly attracted.

Today Rebecca and Ryan have fraternal twins who are eight years old, and she leads a fast-paced life. The twins have learning issues and are quite temperamental. To complicate matters, her husband had a son out of wedlock, a young teen who lives in a nearby town and stays with them every other week.

I have seen Rebecca and Ryan several times in couples sessions. Ryan is quite self-absorbed, drinks too much, and needs constant adulation. He has little interest in the children, although he clearly favors his first son, as he imagines he will be the athlete Ryan never was.

When Rebecca met Ryan, she idealized him. Idealization is a cognitive distortion that biases an individual's ability to see the truth. Impressed with Ryan's looks, his money, and his sociability, she concluded he had a good character. When our longings for love are deep and our stress level is high, the likelihood of biased perceiving is significant. And once a sexual relationship begins, the likelihood of clear thinking diminishes.

This story is unfortunately quite typical. Rebecca had created a negative schema with her self-denigrating comments. This led to the cognitive distortion of *minimization*, downplaying Ryan's faults as she idealized him.

Even though Rebecca is very unhappy, the greatest tragedy of her marriage is the effect her husband is having on his children. His minimal interest in the children is obvious to many, even his own parents. He does get very involved, however, in the issue of their son's weight. Ryan grew up as the chubby kid who was made fun of, and he cannot stand anyone who is overweight. He chides the eight-year-old boy, calls him fat to his face, and blames Rebecca for not managing his diet correctly and not forcing him to exercise. This incredible bind has frozen Rebecca into a position of chronic stress. She is afraid to live with Ryan and yet afraid to leave him, as she fears his anger and retribution.

> When our longings for love are deep and our stress level is high, the likelihood of biased perceiving is significant.

THE EFFECTS OF CLOSED-MINDED RELATING

Recent research has confirmed that emotional trauma, including verbal abuse, causes physical changes in the brain that cause depression and anxiety later in life. The effects of living with someone who is constantly angry and demeaning are cumulative. A high level of the stress hormone cortisol literally kills neurons in the emotional and memory centers of the brain (the amygdala and hippocampus). These changes limit creative thinking, which may be one reason that abused individuals stay in destructive situations.

To relate in an open-minded manner, you need a partner committed to openness and tactful, truthful relating. If you do not understand how your longings and your history govern your perceptions and the negative schemas you have created, you are doomed to repeat harmful patterns from your early life. To come to a truthful, nonbiased view of ourselves, we cannot work alone: we need feedback from a consensus of trusted people who will be honest and straightforward with us. We need to be in reciprocal relationships where we provide the same feedback for those close to us: in essence, relationships built on mutual empathy.

Rebecca had the courage to attend one of my group sessions focused on balanced living. The group consists of ten people who have suffered from inordinate stress. At the beginning of the session, there is typically a degree of stress as people rush in from their jobs, taking care of their children, or other obligations. At the conclusion, there is an air of calm that is deeply health-promoting. The participants look forward to returning the following week, and they come to know each other very well. What happens? As these people receive feedback about who they are from the other objective, well-intentioned individuals in the group, the old story they wrote with a biased pen dissipates, and they begin to see who they are. Authenticity reduces stress and produces faith in oneself and in the potential to grow and learn.

THE BEGINNING OF A NEW STORY

As Rebecca gave feedback to others, many of her suggestions to reduce stress were highly appreciated by group members. As a result, she has seen that she has value: her experiences with avoidance and the stress it produced have helped others. When we give in meaningful ways, when we are recognized for our efforts, we change on a neurochemical level. We feel better because as human beings, we are programmed to help others, not hurt them. We are programmed for empathy, kindness, and compassion. The strength of vulnerability has led Rebecca out of the prison she had been living in. She realized slowly but surely that good people valued her humanness.

> Authenticity reduces stress and produces faith in oneself and in the potential to grow and learn.

Stressed people, especially those accustomed to doing too much, often feel uncomfortable letting others know how they are feeling. "No one wants to hear my complaints over and over again," they may say. It's true that those close to you do not want to hear you complain day after day, but often stressed people think they are complaining when they are really just asking to be understood. There is a profound difference between the honest and reciprocal efforts of people trying to genuinely understand each other and the self-absorption of those who just want to complain and vent. If you chose good people to be close to, they want to hear about your struggles. In fact, if you don't let them in, they will likely drift away. However, you have to give in order to be given to.

Rebecca gave when she thought she had nothing to give, and as a result, she in turn was given a gift that has begun a process of renewal for her. Rebecca realized that her ability to listen empathically was a great asset. Human beings love to be listened to and understood. If you know how to listen, you will always have friends. When we employ empathy, we slow down and become attentive in a way that makes others feel heard and understood. This is the heart of meaningful friendships and a key factor in lessening stress.

STRESSLESS LOVE

When Rebecca stopped focusing on what was wrong with her, she started realizing what has always been *right* about her. One of the greatest accomplishments of our minds is the ability to perceive others and ourselves accurately. This ability is the key to reducing stress and increasing resilience. Eventually Rebecca decided to leave her husband, and today she is living with her children in a small condominium. She has less money and more to do than before, as she works part-time and cares for her twins with very little help from her husband. Yet despite her many responsibilities, she has formed a relationship with a good, caring man, and she is able to love without the stress she continually experienced in her marriage.

You don't need to necessarily be in group therapy, like Rebecca, to rewrite your story, but you do need to be open to the feedback you receive from those close to you. If you are direct, honest, and empathic with others, you are quite likely to receive the same response from them. Empathy is always a reciprocal process. The giving and receiving of empathy is key to reducing stress.

JOURNAL QUESTIONS

- Would you ever make any of the prejudiced comments at the beginning of the chapter?
- Do you have prejudices unique to your experiences?
- What difficulties have you encountered in letting go of your distortions?
- Give an example of being empathic in an interaction with friends or family.

TAKE ACTION

Ask a close friend or relative for honest feedback as to how accurate they consider your perceptions to be. Ask for specifics about your negative biases and prejudices.

CHAPTER 10

Emotional Learning
Hurts That Never Heal

Pain has a way of clipping our wings and keeping us from being able to fly...and if left unresolved for very long, you can almost forget that you were ever created to fly in the first place.

WILLIAM PAUL YOUNG, *The Shack*

People are often surprised when they can't seem to overcome hurts of the past. We need to keep in mind that the brain is biased to remember occasions when we have been hurt in order to protect us from going into the lion's den once again. We record our hurts in the emotional center of the brain, which means our perceptions about hurtful situations are influenced by our feelings. We see them through the lens of our emotions, and we mistakenly believe that we are seeing the objective truth.

We are all storytellers. Early in life, we create stories about ourselves that remain with us and forge our destiny. These stories are based on what we think is being reflected back to us by those around us. If the significant people in our lives have biases of their own, we are looking into a distorted mirror. As a result, our internal story will be mostly fictitious. The following story is an example of the consequences of positive and negative mirroring and how a child can be conditioned to feel anxious, stressed, and fearful. I am telling this story because it is an excellent example of how a person who has absorbed significant hurts can change their negative view of themselves and their cynicism about the world and emerge with a new positive spirit and internal voice. This story exemplifies the power of empathic relationships to uncover the goodness within a person that has lain dormant due to the stressful effects of loss, abandonment, and rejection.

A LITTLE GIRL'S BROKEN HEART

Laura's father died when she was fifteen, leaving her to be raised by her mother and her brother and sister, who were six and four years older, respectively. Laura felt abandoned by her father's death, wondering why her dad would leave her when she was already so anxious after her parents' divorce the previous year.

Anxiety, particularly when paired with the fear of being abandoned, can produce dramatic stress. Laura is now an adult, but the memories of that traumatic time have left her with a biased way of perceiving the present and the past. Whenever she faces a uncertainty — when applying for a new job, applying to graduate school, or dating someone new — she becomes stressed. She suffers from the cognitive distortion of *overthinking:* obsessive ruminations that she believes will result in problem-solving insights.

Even though Laura is quite bright, she has great difficulty discerning facts without the old story of her youth interfering. She is quite familiar with cognitive behavioral therapy and has read several books on CBT and completed the exercises. Nevertheless, when a stressful situation occurs, she falls back into her old, preconceived ideas. Awareness is the first step in rewriting old stories, but it is not enough. An intellectual insight does not change our emotional conditioning. To first understand her experiences, she needed the empathy of those she could

Awareness is the first step in rewriting old stories, but it is not enough.

trust. Only then was she able to place her past hurts in realistic perspective. Trust sets the stage for taking in alternative points of view from people we see as rational, objective, and caring.

The trust that establishes the foundation for open relating is not limited to the relationship between a therapist and client but can exist between family members, friends, or colleagues — or even between a person and a process. For example, you probably have developed sufficient trust in the words in this book to explore aspects of your thinking.

Growing up in a tension-filled home led Laura to certain beliefs about herself that are unsubstantiated today but nevertheless dominant in her thinking. As a result, Laura tends to make decisions about herself and situations she encounters very quickly, without much conscious thought.

Automatic thoughts are immediate, spontaneous thoughts that reflect how you see yourself and your world. They are a common cognitive distortion that is linked to emotional learning, which takes place involuntarily, regardless of objective facts. When we feel strongly, we record certain situations in the light of the emotions of the moment. For example, when we are hurt, we are prone to exaggerations like "He doesn't like me" and "She thinks I'm dumb." Restructuring your self-talk with new awareness of the emotions that support irrational beliefs will allow for a more factual, objective view of life and of yourself.

> Restructuring your self-talk with new awareness of the emotions that support irrational beliefs will allow for a more factual, objective view of life and of yourself.

When Laura first called me, she said she was very stressed and couldn't sleep, and she wondered if I thought talking with her would help. She said a local physician had prescribed an antianxiety drug, but "it made me feel weird, and I was skeptical because he didn't really know me. He prescribed two medications within a twenty-minute visit!" The physician had recommended that she see me, but she was obviously wondering if I would be any different. I tried to address these concerns by telling her that I didn't think I could come to any conclusions about her in a first meeting, and I would look to her to let me know what was bothering her rather than making any premature judgments. I also told her that I imagined it must have been quite disappointing to go for help and feel misunderstood so quickly. These comments seemed to comfort her; her speech slowed, and I thought we had made a connection. We make meaningful connections by sensing what would calm and comfort the other person. It is important to practice this way of perceiving daily to make it become a habit.

Upon first meeting Laura, I was struck by how shy, anxious, and timid she seemed. Once she began speaking, however, it was apparent she was quite intelligent and mature for her twenty-three years.

I asked her if she minded if I asked some historical questions. She immediately began telling me of her childhood and the reasons her mother thought I could be of help to her. She matured early, she told me. "I was not the prettiest girl, not athletic, but I studied and studied and got good grades, even though I was always stressed and worried in every course I took."

Her father was diagnosed with lung cancer when she was in grade school. He suffered through a long series of treatments, including chemotherapy, radiation, and experimental drugs. Laura began to cry as she told me about watching her father's suffering. "I never really thought he would die. I just kept thinking it would be okay, as my mother would convince me that the next treatment was the one that would cure him. She seemed so convincing." Laura told me that her father was a respected football coach in her high school, and she was obviously proud of all the glowing stories she heard about his influence on students.

> We make meaningful connections by sensing what would calm and comfort the other person. It is important to practice this way of perceiving daily to make it become a habit.

Her father's condition worsened at the end of her freshman year, and high school became very difficult for her. She tried to escape through academics and studying the piano. At one point, her pediatrician called her mother thinking that she had developed an eating disorder, as her weight had dropped significantly. "The doctor couldn't understand that I was only 114 pounds because I was too *anxious* to eat, not because I didn't want to eat. You know how it is: you feel sick to your stomach with anxiety, you lose your appetite, your stomach shrinks, and it gets harder and harder to eat." She worried about her father's dying every day, and she felt she couldn't escape the constant questions at school from the teachers who knew her dad.

Shortly after Laura's father died, in the fall of her sophomore year, Laura's mother decided to move back to Massachusetts from Florida. Because Laura wasn't told of the plan until the summer, she felt betrayed. She described how her good nature became submerged as she felt left alone to grieve. She felt constantly stressed and had difficulty sleeping, eating, and relaxing.

When her mother moved to Massachusetts, Laura stayed in Florida with an aunt for her sophomore year and then joined her brother and mother at age sixteen. She felt estranged from her mother, and they never quite regained their old level of closeness. She remained friendless, anxious, and full of distrust of peers and adults. When she entered college, her anxiety worsened, turning into "a suspicious fear of everybody for a while." She continued to excel in class and dated a little, but she remained extremely self-conscious about her intelligence and her physical appearance. This preoccupation turned into an obsessive condemnation of her body, which caused her to feel stressed before every social occasion.

As Laura's anxiety worsened in college, she began to drink more. Hanging out with a few friends with whom she drank on weekends, she finally felt she was developing a sense of belonging.

Unfortunately, alcohol became a habitual way to find relief from her stress and anxiety.

As time went on, Laura became more comfortable with me. She began to be calmer, less judgmental, and more open to other possibilities and to telling me her fears. Empathic relating creates calming brain chemicals that make it easier to recognize and change cognitive distortions to realistic assessments of yourself and others.

Our conversations were always interesting and challenging for me. She would question me frequently as to the validity of psychological principles. She had an air of defeat in the way she related, assuming the worst so she could be prepared for disappointment, regularly employing the cognitive distortion of *magnifying* (accenting your mistakes and perceiving problems as more significant than they are in reality). Any current slight, intentional or not, would be associated with her memories of her disappointing past. She was quick to judge when hurt.

> Empathic relating creates calming brain chemicals that make it easier to recognize and change cognitive distortions to realistic assessments of yourself and others.

As Laura began to feel more comfortable with me, she exposed her vulnerability without the suspicious defenses she usually employed. I told her that if she could learn to trust again, and give up her cynical view of people, she would be able to return to the open heart she once had as a child. She could begin to feel the warmth and support of the people in her life today. Laura cried that session, and from that point our discussions became more meaningful. She was ready to take the insights she had acquired and use them as a basis for applying cognitive behavior therapy.

Laura was learning that she could progress by correcting the distorted views she had of herself and by engaging empathic others to help her see the truth in interactions. The hurts of the past were diminishing.

THE STRENGTH OF VULNERABILITY

One of Laura's major stressors was initiating friendships. She had been deeply wounded in high school, and she carried those scars with her into early adulthood. Although she feared a return to earlier days of self-consciousness about her body, she took a chance and joined a local health club. She has connected with women in her spin classes and has gone out with them on occasions without significant anxiety. She landed her first job as a first-grade teacher, and by all accounts, she is quite loved by her little students and their parents.

She often asks me questions about how to manage particular classroom situations with troubled children and their various personality dynamics. I am continually impressed with how empathic she is to her students and how she intuitively knows how to guide them through self-doubt to better feelings about themselves. When our empathy is expanded and expressed, we are often able to effectively teach aspects of life we ourselves have struggled with and resolved. Laura's major difficulty in her current role is being able to tolerate criticism, as she continues to assume that if she disappoints anyone, it will fracture relationships, and people will abandon her. Despite this anxiety, she manages to do her job well and has earned the respect of her peers and principal.

> When our empathy is expanded and expressed, we are often able to effectively teach aspects of life we ourselves have struggled with and resolved.

As our sessions continued, it was clear that Laura had not only begun to trust me but also started to socialize and open up with some of her coworkers. She met a man at the health club whom she has come to trust. Although she initially felt stressed before every date, she has now settled into a comfortable place with him, allowing herself to feel and be romantic. "It's hard to believe he accepts and loves me!" she told me. "He knows I'm easily stressed, but it doesn't seem to matter that much to him. We get past it and still have fun." Of course, I reminded her that she is not at all hard to be with; this old view of hers is a distorted image we are in the process of correcting.

THE FORMULA FOR BREAKTHROUGHS

So what are the points we want to remember in Laura's transformation? I think she is slowly learning that she is beautiful both inside and outside, something she has never believed about herself. She is beginning to realize that loss, when unattended to, becomes a cynical force within us. Laura never dealt with the loss of her father, her estrangement from her mother and siblings, or the anxiety she felt with peers. She ran away from her own sadness — understandably, because she didn't have a trusted soul to help her work through her grief. She didn't realize that continual running away was creating stress and anxiety that interfered with accurate perception. Her unresolved hurts set the stage for cognitive distortions that she came to believe were real.

When you rediscover the truth, you will likely be more focused on what is right about you and stop the constant search to find out what is wrong with you. Your stress and anxiety will lessen.

We don't do very well when we try to resolve our hurts alone. When we have the courage to open up and find people we trust to genuinely help us by giving us honest feedback, we unleash the impediments to our biased theories. This is the process cognitive behavioral therapists label as uncovering our *core beliefs:* strongly held, often rigid beliefs established early in life.

Laura discovered that she was living according to a set of core beliefs that only reinforced her dismal view of herself and the world. She is in the process of freeing herself of these distortions, and you can, too. When you rediscover the truth, you will likely be more focused on what is right about you and stop the constant search to find out what is wrong with you. Your stress and anxiety will lessen. You will likely return to the sense of peace that has lain dormant, buried under the accumulated hurts of your life.

JOURNAL QUESTIONS AND RESOURCES

- What aspects of Laura's story most affected you?
- What memories does Laura's story stimulate in you?
- Have you talked to those close to you about these experiences?
- Can you identify the hurts in your life that triggered your anxiety?
- What are you doing to understand and resolve those hurts?
- Do you relate to Laura's difficulty in trusting and being close to others?
- Do you believe you can unlearn your tendency to be suspicious?
- To what degree has anxiety interfered with your ability to love?
- Do you have the courage to experiment with love?
- If not, what steps can you take to be more open with those close to you?
- Do you find it easier to be close to pets than people? If so, why?
- Do your stress levels often drive your tendency to generalize from past experiences?
- Do you make diligent efforts to separate the past from the present?

COGNITIVE DISTORTIONS

The following cognitive distortions led Laura to biased perceiving and stress. Record how you have used each, and note in your journal how you will correct this tendency.

- Magnifying
- Overthinking

Also record in your journal:

- Problem-solving insights
- Core beliefs discovered

TAKE ACTION

Try to share your notes with someone close to you, and ask for their honest feedback.

CHAPTER 11

Empathy, Self-Care, and Well-Being

> Biases and quirks of the mind play an important role in consolidating
> our beliefs, but they are also said to influence how happy and
> how healthy we are.
>
> ELAINE FOX, *Rainy Brain, Sunny Brain*

This chapter focuses on the correlation between how we perceive and how we take care of ourselves, with an example of a woman who came to understand and change her distorted view of herself and others through the giving and receiving of empathy in positive relationships. Most people know what they need to do to take care of themselves, but few understand how their thinking and conditioned learning creates resistance to doing so.

Stress has direct effects on our physical as well as our mental health. The United States is the most educated nation in the world when it comes to nutrition and exercise, yet 30 percent of girls and boys in this country are overweight. The Americas have the highest percentage of obesity (26 percent for adults) in the world, according to the World Health Organization. The incidence of type 2 diabetes has skyrocketed not only for adults but also for children and teens, from 5 percent in 1994 to roughly 20 percent in recent years.[1]

As we've been learning, false beliefs, inaccurate perceiving, and a negative self-voice produce stress. Stress causes an imbalance in the amount of the stress hormone cortisol in the body. This imbalance throws off blood sugar levels, causing fat cells to enlarge. Stress and weight gain are highly correlated. This is not a problem unique to the United States: recent studies at the Children's Hospital in Rotterdam indicate that obese children as young as age 8 have elevated levels of cortisol.[2]

OVERCOMING YOUR OWN RESISTANCE

It is easy to tell people how to reduce stress: get regular aerobic exercise, eat a healthy, plant-based diet, get enough sleep, and maintain high-quality, empathic relationships. Sounds simple, right? Yet many people find this advice very difficult to implement with consistency. When we are stressed and depleted, self-care goes out the window. In order to improve our self-care, we have to change our internal voice and see ourselves and other people and situations accurately.

> Stress causes an imbalance in the amount of the stress hormone cortisol in the body. This imbalance throws off blood sugar levels, causing fat cells to enlarge. Stress and weight gain are highly correlated.

When we are stressed, we are vulnerable to making unhealthy choices. A recent study from the University of Zurich discovered that even moderate stress can change the brain chemistry that influences self-control.[3] Participants exposed to an ice bath, which produced moderate stress, chose to eat unhealthy foods. When we are stressed, we crave comfort from sources like sweets or high-fat foods. To make matters worse, our bodies hold on to fat when we are stressed. If this pattern continues, it alters our sensations of feeling full, slows our metabolism, and makes us crave more sugar and fatty foods. It is a vicious cycle. Stress hormones have also been linked to inflammation, which contributes to long-term physical health problems.[4]

Why do we fall into these self-destructive patterns? Eating ice cream releases dopamine, the neurochemical that plays a major role in experiencing reward and pleasure. Hugging someone you love releases oxytocin. Jogging releases endorphins and serotonin. All these chemicals produce happiness: some have only a short-term effect, and others are more lasting. When we don't know how to release these chemicals to give ourselves rewards — for example, through loving interactions with family and friends, by offering a kind word to a stranger, or exercising — we turn to external agents that we associate with pleasure, like sugar, chocolate, nicotine, cocaine, and amphetamines, all of which stimulate the release of dopamine.

REWIRING YOUR BRAIN TO PRODUCE
FEEL-GOOD CHEMICALS

It is important to understand the origin of your thinking and consequent behavior. Otherwise you are likely to blame yourself for being weak-willed, lacking courage, and just being an inferior person. Our coping strategies originate from experience, not from our inabilities.

We learn good and bad self-care habits early in life from those around us. If we observed our parents pour a drink or eat excessively when they were stressed, we are quite likely to mimic their self-care habits. On the other hand, if we saw a parent go down in the basement and get on a treadmill when stressed, we are more likely to exercise to relieve stress. Whatever we learn early as a remedy for life's tensions, whether it's eating ice cream or going for a jog, will create a pathway in the brain connecting this behavior with lightening a bad mood and creating relief. The brain learns from what feels good, and what feels good conditions our thinking in positive or negative directions.

> Our coping strategies originate from experience, not from our inabilities.

Ask yourself what ways of dealing with stress you learned early in life, what biases in perception you created, and how these experiences have influenced the way you talk to yourself.

The good news is that anything that is learned can be unlearned. The developmental psychologist Emmy Werner of the University of California, Davis, conducted a forty-year study of 698 infants born and living on the island of Kauai in Hawaii. The study showed that infants exposed to factors that create high stress — living in an unstable household with a mentally ill mother, for instance — went on to experience more problems like delinquency and poor mental and physical health than those living without these types of risk factors. The startling finding of the study, however, was that one-third of the high-risk children developed into caring, competent, and self-assured individuals. The research team discovered that these resilient children had a strong bond with a caretaker (not a parent) and involvement in a community group or church. Dr. Werner's work, which received national and international awards, proves that we can overcome enormous odds to rewire our brains to live happy and productive lives.[5]

Positive relationships and involvement in meaningful group experiences create resilience and lessen stress. Such experiences stimulate the release of oxytocin, the compassion hormone. This hormone produces feelings of security and calm and inhibits stress and anxiety: thus it protects us against the release of cortisol. In numerous experiments, the neuroscientist Paul Zak has demonstrated the effects of oxytocin on behavior. While cortisol makes us fearful, oxytocin makes us feel comfortable, secure, and in a position to give and receive empathy. When oxytocin levels are high, according to Dr. Zak's research, people's generosity to strangers increases up to 80 percent. The good news is that we can produce this effect with practice by expanding our abilities to communicate with empathy.[6]

> While cortisol makes us fearful, oxytocin makes us feel comfortable, secure, and in a position to give and receive empathy.

MAKING THE CHANGE

What would happen if, instead of reaching for that drink or cookie as you come through the door at night, you kissed your partner passionately? You would release oxytocin and reduce the release of cortisol. The same release would take place if you had a meaningful conversation with a friend, spouse, or child. To make the change, you must initiate these kinds of behaviors.

The stress response inhibits our ability to be empathic. Studies at McGill University by the psychologist Jeffrey Mogil gave subjects the pill metyrapone, a drug that blocks stress hormones. In two separate experiments, they found that empathy increased with the reduction of cortisol. Students were paired with a stranger or a friend and asked to rate the pain of their partner when they submerged the partner's arm in ice-cold water. They displayed more empathy with metyrapone, but they expressed even more empathy when they played a fifteen-minute video game with a stranger before the experiment. Just a shared experience made a difference.[7]

TRICIA'S WAR

Tricia is a corporate manager. She is bright and interesting and has a high degree of empathy for others. She is thirty-six years old, married, with an eight-year-old daughter. She works fifty-five to sixty hours each week and has a forty-five-minute commute home. She has been overweight since adolescence, despite trying many diets. Her long days at work leave her with little energy left to exercise. After feeding her daughter and getting her to bed, she usually zones out watching TV, eating snacks, and having a few glasses of wine to unwind. Her husband, a real estate agent, has a similar work schedule; he is also overweight and eats similarly to Tricia, getting very little exercise.

Tricia's story is a very common one in today's society. She has tried for years to become fit and healthy. However, despite her intellect and her good intentions, she fails repeatedly. Tricia is not mentally ill or depressed, but she is very stressed. She tells me that she doesn't have a single colleague or friend who feels any different.

Tricia has participated in several of my workshops. Over time, she has begun to take care of herself with more consistency. Over the past twelve months, she has lost thirty-two pounds. She seldom consumes simple sugars. She attends an intensive spinning class three times a week and walks a minimum of forty minutes on other days. Her newfound success in taking care of herself has resulted from changing her old internal story to develop a new view of herself.

Tricia, an only child, has been very close to her mother since her parents divorced when she was in middle school. She bonded with her mother over their shared grief and disappointment — and that was when both of them began to gain weight. Weight gain is related to cortisol release. Cortisol causes cravings for carbohydrates, especially sugary sweet foods. It also breaks down muscle tissue, increasing flabbiness. Reducing stress and the release of cortisol is an important step in successful weight loss.

Cortisol causes cravings for carbohydrates, especially sugary sweet foods. It also breaks down muscle tissue, increasing flabbiness.

Tricia has always been a good student. She is successful in the business world and has many friends and a loving marriage, but for many years she carried the view of herself as the "fat girl people talk about later." She suffered from the cognitive distortion of *negative predictions* (overestimating the chances that a behavior or action will have a negative outcome), beginning every day assuming that she couldn't do anything about her weight or her lack of energy. She expected to be unsuccessful in taming her unhealthy eating habits.

As Tricia engaged others in our group sessions, she realized that people truly like her: they find her warmth and ability to refrain from judgment very appealing. Her empathy for others is so apparent that other members have told her they wish they could read people as accurately. They notice how she refrains from quick assessments and that she learns the facts before drawing conclusions about issues or individuals. Initially, she had difficulty accepting compliments, falling prey to the cognitive distortion of *ignoring the positive* (dismissing any positive information and always taking a negative view of situations), but as time went on she let go of her preconceived ideas of herself and opened her eyes to new possibilities.

The support of group members also helped Tricia overcome her fear of conflict, which we came to learn was the core issue for her and a major source of stress. Her dad was prone to angry outbursts, and she always feared his temper and felt uneasy in his presence. These experiences made her fear even the slightest conflict. She expected people to be unreasonable if she had any difference of opinion with them. Her mother avoided her father's wrath by being conciliatory, and later she soothed herself with simple sugars.

Tricia has developed the courage to speak more openly when differences occur. The empathy among group members has allowed her to leave her biases behind and perceive more accurately. She is less inclined toward *mind reading* (assuming she knows what other people are thinking) when she senses conflict. She has gained the confidence to express herself, even when she has differences of opinion with other people. She now experiences less stress, and her energy levels have increased so that she can maintain the more active and healthy lifestyle that had previously seemed elusive. She is not completely out of the woods, but she is on the path to reasonable self-care, and she is learning that her value as a human being extends far beyond her appearance and body type.

As Tricia has begun to feel understood and genuinely cared for, she has been able to use objective feedback from others to help her reevaluate her distorted thinking. Follow Tricia's example, and ask for feedback from those close to you if you are using any of the cognitive distortions that Tricia created.

Now that Tricia has begun the process of rewriting her story with empathy as her guide, she is on the road to a balanced, resilient life. She has found the courage to open her heart to new possibilities even if they initially cause her anxiety. She is moving in a positive direction while realizing that this process is a marathon, not a sprint.

THE EXERCISE ANTIDOTE TO STRESS

Taking care of your health, as Tricia is learning to do, is a crucial part of reducing stress. To engage fully in self-care, however, you need to avoid the negative schemas and cognitive distortions you may have used in the past. Review the work you have done so far so you can proceed without being hampered by prior, biased perceptions of yourself and others. The way we think and perceive is key to removing the obstacles to healthy self-care.

It's also important to maintain balance in your self-care. Too much exercise can be damaging. For example, the body releases free radicals after about ninety minutes of continuous exercise; free radicals increase the risk of cancer. We also know that extreme exercise like ultramarathon running can damage your heart and reverse some of the benefits of exercise. New research indicates there is a "Goldilocks zone" of exercise intensity that provides the greatest health benefit. Two large studies over fourteen years followed 661,000 adults. They were divided into groups that exercised for different amounts of time each week, ranging from no exercise to exercising for ten times the current recommended level of 150 minutes per week. As expected, those who did not exercise at all had the highest risk of premature death. The group that exercised moderately, for less than 150 minutes per week, reduced their early death risk by 20 percent; those

> The way we think and perceive is key to removing the obstacles to healthy self-care.

who met the 150-minute guideline reduced their risk by 31 percent. Tripling the recommended amount of exercise saw the greatest reduction of risk, 39 percent. Above that level, however, benefits tailed off. The group that exercised more than ten times the recommended amount had the same risk reduction as those exercising for 150 minutes per week. The intensity of the exercise also had an effect. Those who exercised more intensely than walking were 9 percent less likely to die prematurely than those who exercised at only a moderate intensity.[8]

For people who find it hard to devote much time to exercise, studies published in the *Journal of Applied Physiology* offer some good news: they indicate that high-intensity interval exercise burns more calories in less time with greater benefits.[9]

You don't have to go to a gym. You can simply walk at a moderate pace for ten minutes to warm up, and then walk as fast as you can for thirty seconds and return to your normal pace for sixty to ninety seconds. You can apply the same technique to spinning, elliptical machines, or outdoor cycling or running.

A variety of exercises produces the most effective fitness levels. Interval training combined with two to three sessions of weight training is ideal. Strength training raises your metabolism, because increasing muscle mass increases your metabolic rate. You will continue to burn calories at a higher rate for up to seventy-two hours after your workout. Additionally, strength training helps prevent muscle loss as you age and aids cardiovascular fitness, bone density, blood pressure, blood sugar regulation, and cholesterol levels. All these benefits reduce stress and produce additional energy and a consistent state of well-being.

EATING RIGHT FOR STRESS REDUCTION

As we've seen, stress and unhealthy eating can create a vicious cycle, sapping more and more of our energy, reinforcing negative self-talk, and making us neglect self-care. Paying attention to what we eat can make a huge difference to mental as well as physical well-being. Following a diet with plenty of plant-based protein will likely lessen your stress levels, improve your overall health, and help you maintain a healthy weight. *The China Study*, by T. Colin Campbell, is one of the best books written on the benefits of plant-based diets. The Mediterranean diet, recommended by the World Health Organization, is easily researchable as well. A study published in the *Journal of the Academy of Nutrition and Dietetics* in December of 2013 indicated that meat eaters have the highest body mass index (BMI) and vegetarians and plant-based eaters had the lowest.[10]

Stress-Reducing Foods

In addition to following a generally healthy diet as outlined above, you may find the following foods valuable. They are high in nutrients that can help reduce stress. My clients who have struggled with stress and weight management have found these foods helpful in combating both issues.

Green leafy vegetables: Green leafy vegetables like spinach, kale, and chard contain folate, which produces dopamine. This pleasure-inducing brain chemical helps keep you calm and boosts energy.

Turkey breast: Turkey meat contains high levels of the amino acid tryptophan, which helps produce the pleasure hormone serotonin, the chemical that regulates hunger and feelings of happiness and well-being. Other foods high in tryptophan include nuts, seeds, fish, tofu, lentils, oats, beans, and eggs.

Oatmeal: Complex carbohydrates like oatmeal can help the brain make serotonin, the same substance regulated by antidepressants. Simple carbohydrates like candy stimulate serotonin release but cause a depletion of energy shortly thereafter.

Yogurt: The bacteria in your gut might be contributing to stress. Research has shown that the brain and stomach communicate, which is why stress can inflame gastrointestinal symptoms. In a 2013 UCLA study of thirty-six healthy women, those who consumed probiotics in yogurt exhibited reduced brain activity in areas that handle emotion, including stress, compared to people who consumed yogurt without probiotics or no yogurt at all. Yogurt also contains calcium and protein in addition to probiotics.

Salmon: The omega-3 fatty acids in salmon have an anti-inflammatory effect that can counteract the negative effects of stress hormones. In a study funded by the National Institutes of Health, Oregon State University medical students who took omega-3 supplements had a 20 percent reduction in anxiety compared to the group given placebo pills. The omega-3s can also raise HDL, our "good" cholesterol.[11]

Berries: The antioxidants and phytonutrients contained in berries strengthen your immune system's response to stress and help eliminate stress-related free radicals. According to a recent study by the *Journal of the Academy of Nutrition and Dietetics*, blueberries can lower blood pressure.[12] Blueberries, strawberries, raspberries, and blackberries are high in vitamin C, which is known to lower blood pressure and cortisol levels, according to German researchers.

Pistachios: Pistachios have heart-health benefits and may reduce acute stress by lowering blood pressure and heart rate. The nuts contain key phytonutrients that may provide antioxidant support for cardiovascular health.

Dark chocolate: Research has shown that dark chocolate can reduce levels of stress hormones, including cortisol. In addition, compounds in cocoa trigger the walls of your blood vessels to relax, lowering blood pressure and improving circulation. Varieties that contain at least 70 percent cocoa are most effective. Eat in moderation.

Seeds: Flaxseed, pumpkin seeds, and sunflower seeds are all great sources of magnesium, as are leafy greens, yogurt, nuts, and fish. Magnesium has been shown to help alleviate depression, fatigue, and irritability and to relieve PMS symptoms, including cramps and water retention.

Avocado: Eating avocados can help you feel full, which makes you less inclined to reach for unhealthy snacks when stressed. Avocados contain moderate quantities of omega-3 fatty acids, lutein, vitamin E, folate, and B vitamins. Avocados are also rich in glutathione, which blocks the absorption of fats that cause oxidative damage. They are calorie heavy, however, so eat them in moderation.

Cashews: Cashews contain zinc, an essential mineral that may help reduce anxiety. Low levels of zinc are known to increase anxiety and depression. One ounce of cashews provides 11 percent of your daily zinc requirement. Other zinc-rich foods are oysters, beef, chicken, and yogurt. Cashews are also rich in omega-3s and protein.

Chamomile tea: This tea, according to a study at the University of Pennsylvania, lowers anxiety considerably. Participants with generalized anxiety disorder who were given chamomile supplements for eight weeks, reported feeling calmer and sleeping better.[13]

Bananas: One banana supplies 30 percent of our daily vitamin B6 requirement, which produces calming serotonin. In addition, bananas are high in potassium.

Raisins: Raisins contain potassium, which is important because stress can deplete the body's potassium levels. The polyphenols in grapes reduce blood pressure, which can help combat stress reactions. Potassium regulates and normalizes blood pressure, helps depression and insomnia, and helps you think clearly.

Exercise and a healthy diet are vital tools for self-care. Combined with accurate views of yourself, the ability to perceive accurately, and the faith in yourself to view your stress as resolvable, they can help you establish a stress-free lifestyle. Let's proceed to solidify your gains.

JOURNAL QUESTIONS

- How do you think your typical way of perceiving hinders your self-care?
- How do you talk to yourself that lowers your energy and compromises your mood?
- To what degree are you critical of your body type?
- How objective do you think you are when assessing your body image?
- What can you do to improve your self-care, including nutrition, sleep, relationship, exercise, and work? Record your progress in your journal weekly, and share your results with a person close to you. You might also ask that person to come along with you on this journey.

COGNITIVE DISTORTIONS

For each cognitive distortion discussed in this chapter — *mind reading* and *ignoring the positive* — list the following: activating event (the trigger), belief, consequence (behavioral and emotional), new belief, and new consequence. For example:

Cognitive distortion: Ignoring the positive
Activating event: A friend asks for a loan.

Belief: People only use me for what I can provide; they don't genuinely care about me.

Consequence: Alienation, loss of friendship, loneliness

New belief: Although my friend was ashamed to ask for financial help, she trusted me enough to come to me.

New consequence: Deeper connection with friends; the benefit of not assuming ill-intent on the part of others.

TAKE ACTION

To limit your stress, you need to ask for help. Ask someone close to you to begin an exercise program with you. If you are currently exercising alone, ask a friend or relative to work out with you. Make a plan and commit to each other to walk, cycle, play tennis, or run together regularly.

CHAPTER 12

"Give and You Shall Receive"
How Giving and Goodness Restore Calm

It is well to give when asked, but it is better to give unasked, through
understanding; and to the open-handed, the search for one who shall
receive is joy greater than giving.

KAHLIL GIBRAN, *The Prophet*

Our world is moving faster than ever before, constantly bombarding us with distractions. How can we remain stress-free in the face of cultural pressures to react instantly to communications and demands? We cannot simply turn our backs on the world: as we have seen, being isolated and self-absorbed increases stress. Isolation is a predictor of early-onset illness.

By contrast, we know that people who give are healthier and happier and live longer. Giving of ourselves is a stress reliever that yields immediate emotional benefits, bringing meaning to our lives. One of the simplest ways to give is through empathy. Empathy allows us to enter the world of another. It allows us to take a mental vacation from ourselves, from our worries, our stressors, and our preoccupations. In the process, we make meaningful connections that produce the

Empathy allows us to enter the world of another. It allows us to take a mental vacation from ourselves, from our worries, our stressors, and our preoccupations.

health-giving neurochemicals we need to manage our stress and improve our lives.

Giving and empathy provide us with opportunities to nurture our innate goodness. We display goodness when we are more concerned with the welfare of others (selflessness) than when we are self-absorbed with our own preoccupations. Studies from the Institute of Gerontology at the University of Michigan have confirmed that giving is more powerful than receiving in terms of reducing mortality.[1]

A fascinating study by the psychologist Paul Wink of Wellesley College followed high school students for over fifty years. He concluded that goodness expressed through giving in the teen years predicted good physical and mental health all the way into adulthood.[2]

IT'S IN OUR GENES

We are genetically programmed to thrive by being empathic and altruistic. The human species has survived thanks to its natural inclination to connect, collaborate, and relate. In the last few years, neuroscientists and social psychologists have provided ample empirical evidence for Darwin's assertion that sympathy is our strongest instinct.[3]

> People who help others on a regular basis are ten times more likely to be healthy than people who do not.

By doing good, we not only help others, we help ourselves as well. People who volunteer their time and energy to help others in need are known to experience the pleasurable feeling known as "helper's high." It leads to a release of endorphins that is beneficial to the helper's health. In his classic study of this phenomenon, Allan Luks, director of Big Brothers and Big Sisters of New York City, found that people who help others on a regular basis are ten times more likely to be healthy than people who do not. By adding meaning and purpose to our lives, helping others improves our sense of self-worth and reduces tension.[4]

Researchers at the University of Buffalo studied one thousand people who had experienced highly stressful situations, such as divorce, job loss, or the death of a loved one. These factors correlated significantly with the development of a host of medical problems including cancer, diabetes, back pain, and heart disease. However, among those who spent significant time giving to others, there was no correlation between stressful events and health issues.[5]

Doing good does us good in the following ways:

- It helps us remain members in good standing of our circles of connection and care (including our families, groups of friends, and religious congregations). A connected life is a good and healthy life.

- It allows us to reap the psycho-physiological rewards of intimacy. The stress hormone cortisol rises sixfold in mammals after thirty minutes of isolation: one study showed that helping others predicted reduced mortality due to the association between stress and mortality.

- It increases our connections to others. Generous people are likely to receive more respect from their peers; selfish people elicit lack of regard and are often avoided.

- It induces others to reciprocate. Transcending our own needs and desires in order to tend to the needs and desires of others turns out to be a very effective way of addressing our own needs and desires. The instinctive inclination to match kindness with kindness can pave the way to lasting relationships.

We all benefit from rediscovering goodness and putting it back at the center of our lives. When we are doing good, our lives are good. When our lives are good, we are happy and free of stress. Yet many of us have unwittingly suppressed our goodness as a result of stress. Understanding how we have lost our way and regaining our natural balance through doing and feeling good, by constructively resolving past hurts, is a journey well worth taking.

The irony is that individuals who may think they are interested only in their own happiness still need to contribute to a healthy culture where goodness prevails. When we engage others in an attitude of goodness, we do what we are biologically programmed to do. When we bond through the relational qualities that goodness embodies, we experience a release of oxytocin, the near-magical neurotransmitter with the following properties:

- reduces anxiety and cortisol levels
- helps you live longer
- aids in recovery from illness and injury
- promotes a sense of calm and well-being
- increases generosity and empathy
- protects against heart disease
- modulates inflammation
- reduces cravings for addictive substances
- creates bonding and an increase in trust of others
- decreases fear and creates a feeling of security[6]

In addition to conferring these benefits, knowing how to express goodness makes us more energetic and more resilient. It gives us more skills with which to manage daily living. We are not limited in our pursuits of knowledge, and we are not limited in the array of people we can befriend. Wisdom consists not in pursuing happiness directly, but rather in building a good life on a foundation of goodness. Happiness comes as a by-product of that process. If there is a shortcut to happiness, it is through goodness.

IMPEDIMENTS TO GOODNESS

Although we are all born with the ability to care for others, circumstances often prevent us from doing so. Many of us have suppressed our innate goodness because of personal setbacks. When our hearts are broken, when the stressors of life are overwhelming, we often lose our innate goodness. We are reluctant to open up to others for fear of being hurt again. Our traumas become permanent negative inclinations that define our character and, with it, our destiny. The good news is that we can work on our past hurts and recover what we thought we had lost forever.

A goodness breakthrough happens when we realize that goodness, empathy, and compassion are the most important things in life, and we change our lives accordingly. Goodness breakthroughs remove the obstacles to the proper functioning of our innate positive inclinations.

The role models and situations we are exposed to early in life set the stage for our innate goodness to flourish or wither. If we have experienced extreme misfortunes, such as being bullied, molested, or abused, our hurt shapes our self-perception and our outlook on life. We mistakenly take responsibility for our life-changing adversities, feeling bad for something that in fact is out of our control. Shame and self-loathing usually accompany our sense of helplessness. When those responsible for our care turn out to be perpetrators of violence, or when the peers we look to for validation turn out to be cruel and sadistic, our world becomes smaller and smaller. Bias and distorted thinking then result in a belief that humans cannot be trusted and that the only way to survive is to avoid any unguarded sharing of ourselves. Less traumatic experiences can also impair our natural ability to express goodness. Growing up in a family stressed by financial difficulties, living in an unsafe neighborhood, having sick parents, or being a child of divorce are all circumstances that can squelch goodness and create a stressful way of living.

> Wisdom consists not in pursuing happiness directly, but rather in building a good life on a foundation of goodness. Happiness comes as a by-product of that process. If there is a shortcut to happiness, it is through goodness.

Goodness breakthroughs take place when we:

- acknowledge our emotions, especially fear, anger, and grief
- have the courage to be vulnerable
- express ourselves to those who possess goodness
- absorb feedback without being defensive
- use empathy to understand those who hurt us
- move away from self-absorption and negativity
- forgive ourselves

When we follow these steps (and we may have to repeat them frequently, depending on the depth of the emotional hurts we experienced), we are very likely to return to a basic feeling of goodness. I have worked with many people who have changed the way they talk to themselves. I have seen that changing self-talk results in better self-care, less stress, a better disposition, and ultimately being better to others.

FORGIVENESS AND GOODNESS

No individual reaches adulthood without having made errors in judgment. Yet if we allow these errors to haunt us and determine our self-perceptions, we cannot be accepting of ourselves or of others. Forgiving ourselves is the heart of forgiveness. Forgiveness comes slowly, as we learn from the tragedies and traumas of the past in an effort to transcend them. However, with time and effort, we can move forward, building on the past rather than endlessly repeating it. We can accept our imperfections, learn from our regrettable behavior, and open our hearts to the goodness that has lain dormant under layers of guilt and embarrassment.

The degree to which we can befriend ourselves determines how much we are able to give to the world. Having an understanding inner voice, neither permissive nor punitive, frees up energy to give and to go outward. Self-critical and self-aggrandizing individuals cannot be fully present to others. A widened perspective of forgiveness and realistic appraisal of ourselves opens us up to the richness of the human experience. Research by Robert Enright at the University of Wisconsin indicates that those who score high on an inventory of forgiveness are less likely to be depressed, anxious, hostile, narcissistic, or exploitive and are less likely to become dependent on drugs or nicotine.[7]

FEAR, PREJUDICE, AND GOODNESS

If we have a solid sense of self, we are far more likely to be gracious to groups other than our own. We develop greater openness toward difference when we have been loved, respected, and understood in the early parts of our lives. If we received the empathic resonance that all young people crave, we grow with optimism and excitement about learning new ideas from other people. This process begins in our families. If our parents had a diverse group of friends, if they were open to learning new ideas to replace less functional ones, then we are likely to value and feel happy when learning. By contrast, children who grow up in insecure households learn that the enemy is outside, and that only the people inside are good. Goodness then takes on a distorted meaning, promoting the idea that we should be and do good only to our own, not to those unlike us. This is a formula for living with chronic stress.

Perception and mood are closely related. When we feel understood and secure, we are more likely to perceive accurately and more likely to do good rather than harm.

The results of the World Values Survey show that when we feel secure, bias and prejudice are markedly reduced and happiness is increased.[8] Perception and mood are closely related. When we feel understood and secure, we are more likely to perceive accurately and more likely to do good rather than harm.

Social psychologists have long established that avoidant or anxious individuals bolster their own self-worth by assuming that their group, whether ethnic, religious or otherwise, is superior. This defensive posture creates rigid thinking, the black-and-white perceptions that promote oversimplified theories about human beings and their affiliations.

Rigidity protects a fragile sense of self; it creates an artificial road map that gives an insecure person unreliable answers to life's complexities. Establishing a worldview based on anything but the truth will ultimately create more and more fear and stress. Anxious people tend to avoid new ideas and new ways of thinking. Avoidant people often run from new challenges. Both of these types fear loss of self-esteem if they give up their entrenched beliefs.

To uncover our basic goodness, we must make a disciplined effort. We must recognize that goodness is part of our being: it is at the heart of our humanness. We must move away from excluding anyone from our lives on the basis of bias or prejudice. But what if we have been raised to believe that one group is superior to another, or that our thinking patterns are superior to those of others? If you think your education, race, religion, vocation, income, or location make you superior, then you are profoundly mistaken and doomed to a life of superficial relationships. Goodness is not just for those who adhere to the Judeo-Christian ethic, or the Buddhist or Muslim ethic, or the secular humanist ethic: it is innate to all of us.

We practice goodness by the way we live, not by holding on to fixed ideas that shore up our fragile sense of self. Be honest with yourself. Acknowledge the situations and the people who threaten you. Strive to resolve these issues rather than punishing innocent people for being their authentic selves. This may entail a self-examination that feels risky, but you will never be comfortable in your own skin unless you have the courage to allow yourself to be vulnerable. Only then will you discover where you need to grow and learn. In many instances, we need to unlearn mistaken positions that we have held on to defensively. We are programmed to remember what caused us fear and pain. Fear creates rigid thinking, which leads to false theories, inaccurate judgments, and inordinate amounts of stress. Reevaluate your past with today's wisdom, and in the process you will release your dormant innate goodness. Thomas Paine, one of our Founding Fathers, once said, "My country is the world, my religion is to do good." Our world would surely be a better place if we could all live by his words.

We probably all remember our parents telling us to "be good." Those of us who were raised in one of the major religions remember being told to "do good" by serving others. Over time, these phrases have been taken for granted and seem to have lost their basic message. Goodness makes our world a better place because human beings are kinder to each other when we feel safe and secure. The rise of aggression in our culture, the threat of terrorism, and the increase of bullying in our schools and in our workplaces have created fear. Fear creates anxiety, and anxiety creates distorted thinking. Ultimately, distorted thinking creates an inflexible, oversimplified view of the world. These recent changes in our culture have decreased goodwill toward others and fostered more self-absorption and less giving.

ANGER AND GOODNESS

Anger is a powerful impediment to the flow of goodness. Extensive research has revealed that when people are angry, their attempts to resolve conflict are accompanied by the cognitive distortions of *quick judgments* and *oversimplifications*. The stress hormone adrenaline, which is released when we are angry, causes stored memories to become more vivid and harder to erase than less emotional memories.

We are born with the ability to understand and do good, but these natural gifts wither if we perceive in distorted ways. My client Mary (whom we met in chapter 2) struggled with letting go of the earlier hurts in her life. Because she held on to resentments with both fists clenched and had great difficulty giving up her negative schemas, she was blocking any opportunity for love and friendship. Unable to forgive her father for leaving the family, she continued to *generalize* and *ignore the positive* to reinforce her core beliefs, ruining any chance for her inborn goodness to emerge.

Dr. Paul Levine's work demonstrates how even a trauma victim can return to a state of goodness through meaningful contact with an empathic, compassionate individual. His studies support the notion that when grief, trauma, or losses are not resolved, a cynical force activates within us and limits our potential for goodness.[9]

Resolving past hurts may require us to feel and acknowledge sadness. The Boston psychoanalyst Elvin Semrad has said, "Sadness is the vitamin of growth." Sadness forces us to slow down, get back in touch with our true nature and ourselves. It makes us reflect. I continue to be fascinated by how sadness calms a stressed individual, actually relaxing a person's physiology in a way that is visible to any observer.

Mary's anger and her refusal to experience sadness prevented her from seeing goodness in herself or anyone else. Ask yourself if you hold on to anger in any form, preventing you from experiencing and sharing your goodness. We need to take inventory frequently to make sure we are not blocking ourselves from feeling compassion by refusing to face the emotions we find threatening.

By letting go of the misguided beliefs that have supported our distorted view of the world, we light the spirit of basic goodness so that love and compassion can break through. This kind of breakthrough removes the obstacles to seeing our world and ourselves clearly.

GRIEF AND GOODNESS

Goodness breakthroughs occur when we embrace our sadness rather than give in to our natural tendency to avoid and escape discomfort. The grief we all encounter grows within us unless we heed the warnings of sadness. We can recover from the unfortunate yet predictable pains of life if we slow down and become aware of the message that sadness provides. We need to learn how to make our emotional victories an integral part of life.

The story of Randy is an extreme example. Randy is a tough, impatient, highly stressed bank vice president. He has a successful career and home life, but he is usually stressed. His dad died when he was only one year old, and his mother married an abusive man shortly thereafter. Randy's stepfather physically abused his stepchildren but not the two boys he fathered with his first wife. The abuse stopped only when Randy became an adolescent and was mature enough to defend himself.

> We can recover from the unfortunate yet predictable pains of life if we slow down and become aware of the message that sadness provides.

Unlike his siblings, he visited his stepfather on occasion after he became an adult. When his stepfather was diagnosed with advanced pancreatic cancer, Randy took on the job of overseeing his stepfather's care. I asked him, given how he had been treated, what makes him so devoted to his stepfather.

"I feel bad for him," Randy replied. "I realized as we talked that he didn't know any better: he is such a resentful, angry man. Now he is dying alone. I can't stand to think of him being in that home alone and afraid. I feel better knowing I can be with him despite the past. In a strange way, he has given me something. I've learned I'm not such a hard-ass after all."

As a result of this goodness breakthrough with his stepfather, Randy began to give more to others. He has recently been recognized as one of the few business leaders doing good in his community. He has been applauded for his unselfishness and goodness, qualities that he did not previously believe he possessed. As with many goodness breakthroughs, Randy recovered a fundamental aspect of himself that had been hidden, lying below unresolved suffering and limiting his joy and ability to be present with others.

Other stories may be less dramatic than Randy's, but they show other ways in which goodness breakthroughs can result in a life in which goodness is expressed daily. Laura, the teacher who became cynical after her father's long, arduous battle with cancer, rediscovered her natural goodness through the arrival of an impoverished Haitian girl in her classroom. Laura abandoned her self-absorption as she found herself giving to a little girl who had lost her parents and her country. She rediscovered her goodness as she witnessed her new student's courage to grieve her losses and move on. How could this little girl display such empathy and compassion to her classmates after such tragedies? She simply had the ability to be vulnerable, to cry, to talk, and to express all that rocked her body and mind. The teacher in this case was the student. The lesson was one of how good grief returns us to doing and feeling good.

> Once we have traveled back and healed our broken hearts, we can see the world differently. We can see ourselves and others clearly, and we notice the good in life again.

Once we have traveled back and healed our broken hearts, we can see the world differently. We can see ourselves and others clearly, and we notice the good in life again. Suddenly, we appreciate the person who holds the door open for us or the smile of a crossing guard directing traffic in the morning, and we are warmed by watching the kiss and embrace of a mother and child saying good-bye for the day as the school bus door opens. A breakthrough has occurred, and we are in a position to express and share goodness with others once again.

THE GOODNESS FORMULA

Laura's story provides a clear formula for the release of goodness and the decrease of stress. We need a role model, someone who expresses or exemplifies goodness. The little girl in Laura's classroom showed the courage to address grief, sorrow, and disappointment. In essence, she was able to face her troubles, not run away from them as people so often do. Despite her life circumstances, she possessed the ability to be empathic with a new, diverse group of children and to relate to them with an open mind. She could have developed various cognitive distortions to support and maintain her hurts and turn them into permanent resentments, but instead she was able to perceive accurately and without bias. As a result, she remained free of stress.

Laura was able to experience a goodness breakthrough by following the path of her young student. She faced up to her sorrow and disappointment in losing her father. She discovered the strength of vulnerability, confided in friends, and discovered the way to go on with grace.

Our cognitive powers are at their best when we are emotionally healthy. We think more clearly and return to more accurate ways of perceiving. We experience what the psychologist Richard Tedeschi of the University of North Carolina calls "post-traumatic growth." In other words, out of loss comes gain.[10] Once we have begun to recover from our darkest hour, we see the world differently. We want to share our internal sense of goodness with everyone. Our perception of our world and of human nature changes for the better, and this change opens us up to happiness again.

There is no doubt that goodness is good for us, and if the hurts of our past have made us lose sight of our internal goodness, we can take steps to regain and refocus on this amazing ability. Goodness retrieved gives us the opportunity to improve and extend our lives while also enabling us to contribute to a better society and world.

JOURNAL QUESTIONS

- What relationship do you think goodness has to your stress level?
- What past hurts do you think keep you in a state of stress that you have been unable to let go?
- What aspects of Mary's story do you relate to?
- What aspects of Randy's story do you relate to?
- What aspects of Laura's story do you relate to?
- What is your plan to resolve any of the impediments to goodness you recognized in your own experience while reading this chapter?

COGNITIVE DISTORTIONS

For each cognitive distortion discussed in this chapter — *overgeneralizing*, *quick judgments*, and *oversimplifications* — list the following: activating event (the trigger), belief, consequence (behavioral and emotional), new belief, and new consequence. For example:

Cognitive distortion: Overgeneralizing
Activating event: My wife agreed with my boss when I told her how he reacted to me.
Belief: She thinks I'm incompetent.
Consequence: Dejection, moody behavior, withdrawal
New belief: She was just being honest. I realize she was trying to help: I know I can't go to work late continually and not expect a reaction.
New consequence: I am learning to not make assumptions based on very little information.

TAKE ACTION

Commit to one act of goodness every day, and note how you feel in your journal. Record your stress level after you engage in giving behavior. Try to come out of yourself, extend yourself, and reap the benefits of giving.

CHAPTER 13

I Am Who I Am
How Authenticity Soothes the Soul

Perhaps I can say that I am a bit astute, that I can adapt to circumstances,
but it is also true that I am a bit naive. Yes, but the best summary,
the one that comes more from the inside and I feel most true is this:
I am a sinner whom the Lord has looked upon.

POPE FRANCIS, interview with Fr. Antonio Spadaro, August 19, 2013

Fritz Perls, the founder of Gestalt psychotherapy, often recited the following to encourage authentic relating: "The psychotic person says, 'I am Abraham Lincoln'; the neurotic person says, 'I wish I were Abraham Lincoln'; the healthy person says, 'I am who I am.'" Psychologists and spiritual leaders have often encouraged people to discover their true self and to have the integrity to be true to their beliefs and values. This is often referred to as the difference between the "false" self and the "real" self, the difference between authenticity and pretense. When we replace our inherent personality with one that is trying to please in order to gain acceptance, approval, and love, we lose our soul.

> When we replace our inherent personality with one that is trying to please in order to gain acceptance, approval, and love, we lose our soul.

In order to live your life with balance and calm, you must partake in an ongoing quest to know yourself. If you do not know the truth about yourself, you will not find sustainable love. You will not succeed in life without considerable stress. We create a tension arc within ourselves when we can't relax and be ourselves. Somewhere within, we all want to reveal ourselves to the world and feel accepted and acknowledged for our unique being. When we are afraid to let go and be real, it is often because we harbor the fear that if others find out the truth about us, we will be rejected. At the very least, we will not be seen as a desirable person to be in a relationship with.

I have known many people over the years who are respected and revered by others but feel like a fraud inside. They hide their doubts and insecurities and believe that nobody sees that side of themselves. They are afraid that if they reveal their whole selves, they will not seem as attractive to others.

One of my clients, Tony, is unusually quick-witted and is often the life of the party. The irony is that he hates parties. "I have to get so energized to get up for going, and it just isn't worth the effort. When I leave a social gathering, I am exhausted because it's show time. It's all an act to make people like me. I am so stressed that before I go, I have to have a few drinks just to get in the car and tolerate the fear of being found out once again."

If you met Tony, you would see a tall, handsome, well-spoken, and warm individual whom you probably would immediately like. But even if you told him that you liked him, it would not sink in. His internal voice continually tells him that he is not that smart, not that attractive. If he weren't trying so hard, people wouldn't like him.

Emily, another client, could be his counterpart. She is intelligent, compassionate, attractive, and engaging. However, she also suffers from the belief that if people really knew about her struggles, they would feel differently about her. She grew up without a father. Her mother married three times and divorced each husband after a few years. Needless to say, Emily's upbringing was anything but stable. She has always felt embarrassed about her past, trying desperately to hide the troubled world she came from. Her self-talk is punitive, demanding more and more from her, not allowing her to relax and just be. She always has a to-do list in her pocket and is trying to achieve as much as possible on any given day so that she can feel accomplished and successful.

Tony and Emily are not mentally ill. They are both capable, interesting, caring people who most people enjoy being with. If you met them, you would probably not realize how stressed they are. Why do they feel so stressed and so afraid to expose more of who they are?

THE OLD STORY

By now it should be clear that we all create a story about ourselves early in life. The mirrors we look into give us a sense of who we are and what capabilities we possess. If the mirrors we look into are distorted, we write a distorted account of who we are, and these thoughts become embedded in our sense of self. A lack of empathy early in life creates an unsupportive internal story, which sets the stage for overdoing, overachievement, and stress as we attempt to make up for what we secretly feel is missing.

This tendency is extremely common among people who are admired on the outside but feel fraudulent on the inside. People like Tony and Emily, who have the capabilities to achieve and provide, come to believe that in order to maintain their self-worth, they have to hide their vulnerabilities and continually overachieve to maintain their positive image.

To rewrite these distorted stories, they need feedback from caring, rational people, people who will tell them who they are from an objective point of view. When you are open to the empathy of those you trust, you begin to develop stronger relationship skills and expand your own empathic range. Your story becomes an authentic biography that allows you to shed the weight of the past and move forward with self-assurance, inner calm, and faith in yourself.

INNER- VERSUS OUTER-DIRECTED

The constant pressure to perform that people like Emily and Tony feel creates a perpetual stress response. Once this way of living becomes entrenched, it reinforces the cognitive distortion that people will love and respect you only if you perform well and please them. Ironically, the opposite tends to be true. Most people are attracted to authenticity: it relaxes us because we realize that we don't have to be on guard — we can be human, have flaws, and make mistakes and still be accepted and liked.

When we are directed by our internal values, attitudes, experiences, and ideas, we are able to determine our life's course (within reason). Of course, certain factors are out of our control. However, an inner-directed person is usually able to make the best out of unfortunate occasions, as their sense of self-worth usually remains intact.

Outer-directed people tend to feel that their fate is in other people's hands. They are strongly influenced by family, friends, organizations, and the situations they encounter. They believe that their life and their ability to feel comfortable in their own skin are controlled by external factors. Of course, if you believe that, then you probably also believe that you are helpless to make any changes.

Emily and Tony are outer-directed despite both being very capable people. They are learning to be aware of their self-talk so that they can catch themselves before they start adjusting their behavior to the whims of others. For the most part, their behavior has been unthinking, an automatic response to the way their nervous system senses what another person wants of them.

The distinction between the false self and the real self is often a product of being outer-directed. The false self is created by the early perception, and the ultimate belief, that those we depend on for emotional sustenance want us to be a certain way. The outer-directed person is afraid that others will be less interested in her, disappointed in her, angry, or all three, if she fails to live up to these external standards.

Children who grow up in these circumstances learn to refrain from expressing themselves spontaneously and genuinely. They learn not to risk the negative reaction of their families. Conforming to established family norms and suppressing what they really experience inside becomes one way of feeling safe and secure. This is a formula for a life of stress.

In contrast, the real self emerges in an environment where caregivers are strong enough to allow for differences of opinion, taste, and interests without judgment. In this type of environment, a child is free to explore and experience the trials and errors of learning without criticism and with parental love and support. This is a formula for a life of emotional freedom.

SELF-KNOWLEDGE

Tony and Emily struggle with the same difficulty — the fear of being found out. Both are continually trying to put points on the scoreboard to prove that they are worthwhile. They find it hard to believe that people will accept and appreciate them, and perhaps even like them more, when they are not trying so hard to perform. Their desire to prove themselves worthy creates an environment that feels stressful to all involved.

On occasion, we all disguise our true feelings for self-protection. We may need time to understand given situations and individuals. This response becomes a problem only when it becomes second nature, a characteristic way of relating. We then lose our authenticity. Our natural being lies dormant until we make consistent efforts to uncover the person we really are. Through awareness and the empathy of others, we can expand our self-knowledge, but only

> Through awareness and the empathy of others, we can expand our self-knowledge, but only if we are open to discovery and self-disclosure.

if we are open to discovery and self-disclosure. New emotional habits and ways of being can be established, but they require the courage to practice consistently expressing your authentic self.

BECOMING ONESELF

A friend of mine, Dr. Jim Brennan, wrote a beautiful book called *The Art of Becoming Oneself.* The following paragraph is from his chapter on authenticity.

> When we face difficult life choices, we reduce large amounts of pressure almost immediately by simply remembering who we are. Each of us possesses an inner power that lies not so much in the roles we play, or the circumstances we face, but rather in our ability to be essentially the same person in every situation. If we develop a deep trust in our authenticity, not simply blind trust, but trust based on experience, courage, and self-knowledge, we can make the complicated look simple, the difficult look easy. Some may believe that being the same person in every situation requires us to be firm and inflexible. However, when we observe the people we admire most, we see that what they hold in common is the unusual extent to which they allow their uniqueness to flow freely. They seem to know what is best, what they stand for, and what they deeply need.[1]

Dr. Brennan is surely guiding us to reach deep within and reveal who we are, not what others may want us to be or what we become out of the fear of losing love and respect. Think of the people you respect most in life. What are the qualities they possess? I would guess they are qualities discussed throughout this book. How many tears will be shed at the end of your life? My grandfather left this earth with no one crying; his business success meant nothing in the end. My mother left this earth many years ago, but I still shed tears today. Her warm personality made her lovable. Her open heart enabled her to communicate in a way that calmed and soothed the people she encountered. My mother knew how to listen and make relationships with people from all walks of life.

As a result, even when she was terminally ill, my mother seemed at ease with herself. I often think of a close friend who told me that her own mother, on learning of her terminal diagnosis, said, "I can't bear the thought of how much I will miss my family." Her first thought was of her family, not of work or of her house or her possessions. What will your first thought be when the time comes? What have you devoted your life to? Will you leave this world knowing you allowed your unique self to flourish? Or will you leave this world knowing that you became whatever it took to assuage your anxiety in the moment?

COMING OUT

A few minutes before one of my group sessions, people were discussing Diane Sawyer's interview with Caitlyn (formerly Bruce) Jenner, in which Jenner acknowledged that she felt more like a woman than a man. As I entered the room, one of the men said, "If there is anything I have learned through group sessions it is that we all have to be ourselves." There is no other way to live if you want to be at ease with yourself and everyone else." If, every day, we maintained our true identity and lived our lives according to our beliefs and values, we would increase our levels of happiness and self-respect while reducing our stress levels significantly.

Jenner commented to Diane Sawyer before the interview, "This is going to be difficult." Of course having the courage to be ourselves can be difficult; but ultimately it is not as difficult as wearing a mask throughout life. Authenticity is energizing. Pretending to be somebody we are not is exhausting.

People often do not realize how taxing a false identity is until they uncover their true selves and experience being themselves in several social contexts. Once you experiment with revealing your authentic self, you may find yourself calmer than you ever have been. Every time you take the chance to express yourself honestly and realize your old story is fictional, you reduce stress and lift your spirits. New experiences make new memories and dispel old conditioning. A number of studies in positive psychology examined by Abigail Mengers at the University of Pennsylvania have demonstrated the positive correlation between being yourself, authenticity, recognizing your uniqueness, stress reduction, and overall well-being.[2]

> Every time you take the chance to express yourself honestly and realize your old story is fictional, you reduce stress and lift your spirits.

This transformation can be difficult to make because living with a false self for years blinds a person's ability to see their own potential. They need help identifying the qualities they have buried for fear of rejection, loss of approval, and inability to please others. If they can recognize these qualities, however, a goodness breakthrough can take place, and they can begin to uncover what has been hidden.

Living authentically creates an inner calm and allows us to actualize our potential as we free up energy consumed by the stress of pretending. We can then use our energy to create and relate to others with all we have to give. We are free to be honest and spontaneous, without the self-consciousness that living with a false self produces.

INTIMACY

Once you have applied self-knowledge to correct your distorted self-perceptions, your newfound awareness will likely affect the quality of your relationships. As you feel better about yourself, you will feel more freedom to express yourself openly and honestly. You will have less to hide and will gain the courage to be vulnerable.

Our importance lies in the love we give and the love we receive. Work is important, but when professional achievements become a means to try to undo the hurts of the past, we are doomed to a life of frustration. Whitney Houston's voice and Lance Armstrong's Tour de France wins may never be matched, but obviously, the success of these two people did not resolve their internal angst. Something was wrong inside, not outside. Fame, money, physical beauty, and athletic prowess are not enough to give a person internal comfort. We can achieve a balance of personal and professional success only if the foundation of our personality is centered on our ability to relate and our ability to love. Ultimately, if we succeed at love, we succeed at life.

WHO AM I?

I have a client, Giovanni, who is an exceptionally talented musician and also one of the most empathic people I know. When he gives feedback to people, he is calm and thoughtful. He goes to great lengths to not offend those he is addressing. When he does make a comment, it is usually insightful and factual. As a result, his comments are often received positively even when he is being (constructively) critical.

Giovanni has a wonderful marriage and the respect of many who know him. Yet he also has a very critical inner voice, especially about his music, even though he and I have often discussed all the concepts in this book. One day, as he was listening to his favorite radio show playing several piano pieces, he was impressed. When the DJ announced the pianist's name, it turned out to be Giovanni himself. He immediately became critical. His initial response to the music was objective: without knowing who was playing, he had the distance necessary to see clearly and accurately. The second response, however, was typical of his old self-talk: he's not good enough, he doesn't measure up. His first response was unaffected by past experience; the second, biased response was emotional, based on the hurts of the past.

Giovanni is beginning to realize, through the work he has been doing for the past year, that his old story has robbed him of a joyful, stress-free life. He is aware of the negative biases of his self-talk and the effect of releasing stress hormones. He has become more open to the opinions of others, especially the honest feedback of trusted family and friends. Slowly but surely he is coming to feel less stressed as he uncovers the truth about his abilities and his character.

> Self-knowledge is absolutely necessary to reduce stress and to live according to our true values while maintaining our integrity.

It takes enormous courage and humility to be open to others to find out who we really are. Self-knowledge is absolutely necessary to reduce stress and to live according to our true values while maintaining our integrity. The giving and receiving of empathy and the courage to recognize and eliminate cognitive distortions are the keys to knowing yourself and the people you encounter.

Genuine, authentic relating enlivens the spirit. This gives us the energy and resilience to go into the world, absorb emotional blows, and still come home with our self-respect and integrity intact. Empathic CBT is the vehicle to maintain this perspective.

JOURNAL QUESTIONS

- To what degree do you express yourself honestly to those close to you?
- If you do, what are your fears in the process?
- What would you do differently in your life if you were not worried about other people's judgments?
- What are the emotional and psychological costs to you to live a life based on a false self?
- What career would you find enjoyable if you were not worried about the opinions of other people?

- Would you have married or be with the same significant other if you were making a free choice, independent of the wishes of your family and friends?
- Do you think it is possible to be yourself in this way? Why or why not?

TAKE ACTION

Share your answers to the journal questions in this chapter with two or more close family members or friends. Ask for their truthful opinion of your responses. Record your findings in your journal, and revisit them periodically.

The Power of Deep Connections

> In the communal act of telling and listening, listening and telling,
> the sense of belonging begins.
>
> ERNEST KURTZ AND KATHERINE KETCHAM, *The Spirituality of Imperfection*

Every Friday morning I meet with a group of people in a small church, where we discuss all the themes I have covered in this book. The people who attend don't need to be in therapy; they are not disturbed. They come because they are learning from each other. They are striving to learn how to lead a balanced life with the minimum of stress.

The discussions are unstructured, but inevitably we end up talking about how people relate and perceive. I begin by asking if there are any issues left over from the previous week. Everyone usually smiles and looks around the room as if to say, "We're so busy — who can remember last week?"

One of our witty members says, "It's always safe to say that we talked about relationships, intimacy, authenticity, our biases, and what gets in the way of truly listening." He's right, because these are topics integral to reducing stress and increasing resilience. This past week people were talking about being too busy, always being on the move, and not taking time for themselves. One member, Peter, mentioned that the only time he ever feels calm is about halfway through this Friday morning meeting. I asked him how that comes about. He answered, "I think we really listen to each other. When we slow down to really connect, it is relaxing. It seldom happens in my daily life, but I'm beginning to have these moments with my wife at home. I can really feel the difference physically, like all of a sudden I can just let go and be myself, without any worries."

Angie, a middle-aged mother of two who works full time in a software company, sighed as Peter was talking. "It's great in here — how we listen to, connect, and calm each other. I just find it so hard to take the time at home. I signed up for two yoga classes yesterday. I already feel guilty, like I'm being selfish to take time for myself when there is so much to do at home."

Peter immediately responded, "Absolutely not, you are not selfish! You are letting the rest of the people in your life off the hook. If you take care of yourself, they don't have to take care of you."

The group went on to discuss the point that self-care is never selfish, but it may feel that way when you live a frenzied life. Who has time to exercise, meditate, and still check everything off their to-do list? As the discussion deepened, and people asked more open-ended questions of Angie, she disclosed that her parents seldom praised their children or each other. They worked hard, didn't take vacations, and rarely seemed to have much fun with friends or each other. "My parents were serious people, stiff upper lip, and all that stoic stuff."

As Angie opened up, so did the others in the group. We began to see each person's unique history. We learned how perceptions distorted early in life create misguided lifestyles. Unresolved issues destroy inner calm and can drive us to feel we must always be "on." Many of us do not know how to turn the dial down when it is not necessary to perform. Angie's distorted idea that she needs to be accomplishing something at all times has been creating more and more stress and making it impossible for her to see a way out.

As she and others talked of how to develop a dimmer switch, Peter added that the media fuels the ideas that we must always try to be better and that we can buy happiness and satisfaction. "Every car, cable, and dish TV commercial is telling me a new car, faster Internet speed, and more stations will make my life better. Every gym commercial, every moisturizing cream and shampoo commercial is telling us if we looked better, we would be happier. What a farce — it only makes people more confused about how to live!"

> Unresolved issues destroy inner calm and can drive us to feel we must always be "on." Many of us do not know how to turn the dial down when it is not necessary to perform.

Eventually the discussion returned to Peter's earlier point, that self-care is not selfish. Everyone agreed that he was right but that the idea is not easy to implement. As we talked about how to calm down and to reduce stress, the conversation became more empathic. People were listening attentively and deeply while exploring the unique ways they had each come to be so stressed. The past was brought into the present with new possibilities. Over time, old stories are being revised; each person's novel is becoming a nonfiction book. Childhood distortions are being corrected and replaced with truthful assessments of who each person is today, from the consensus view of people who have connected with each other in meaningful ways every week. Empathic listening creates trust, and this trust deepens connections. This process leads to disclosure and discovery.

This is how empathy works. As defenses fade and new possibilities enliven our spirits, we realize that our health and survival depend on our ability to accurately understand and sensitively respond to each other. Empathy creates a foundation of trust that changes our brain chemistry, calms our soul, and puts us in a position to listen. We can then open up and take in what we need to hear in order to rewrite our story, correct distorted thinking, and at last become who we are destined to be.

I hope you will incorporate empathic CBT into your life and pass on your insight and understanding to all you encounter. Let's make every effort possible to relate with a sense of calm and caring. Our health and happiness depend on our willingness to practice empathic, truth-oriented relating. If we can give this gift to others, we can be part of making a better world.

APPENDIX

Assessment Tools

STRESS QUESTIONNAIRE

The following stress questionnaire is designed to help assess your level of stress so that you can determine what aspects of your life you may need to address more consistently for greater well-being. For each question to which you answer yes, circle the statement's number or list the numbers on a separate piece of paper.

1. Do you tend to overwork and do most things yourself?
2. Do you have difficulty falling or staying asleep?
3. Is your nutrition generally poor to fair?
4. Have you experienced the death of a spouse in the past six months?
5. Have you experienced the death of a close friend in the past six months?
6. Have you been divorced or seeking divorce in the past six months?

7. Do you have a child who has been experiencing serious emotional difficulties in the past year?

8. Has your health deteriorated significantly in the past year?

9. Have you had difficulties in the sexual arena in the past year?

10. Have you or your significant other lost your job in the past year?

11. Do you or your significant other have trouble with a boss?

12. Do you often feel guilty for reasons that you know are irrational?

13. Do you frequently feel impatient when you have to wait in line?

14. Have you been fighting more often with your partner?

15. Do you feel as if you are racing through each day, seldom able to slow down?

16. Do you have few supportive relationships?

17. Do you tend to react more strongly to the normal stressors in life than others you know?

18. Do you wake each day feeling as if you won't be able to cope effectively?

19. Do you have few calm moments during the day?

20. Do you often think you have little time for exercise, relaxation, or letting go?

Scoring

Score one point for each question to which you answered yes.

1–6 points: Low stress

7–12 points: Moderate stress

13–17 points: Significant stress

18 or more points: Extreme stress

EMPATHY QUOTIENT QUESTIONNAIRE

Read the following statements and, as honestly as possible, assess whether each is true for you. For those that are, circle the statement's number or list the numbers on a separate piece of paper. Complete this questionnaire before and after reading this book, and compare your answers.

1. I have been told by more than one person that I lack empathy.
2. I have been told by more than one person that I am empathic.
3. I feel good when I help another person.
4. I don't feel much when I help another person.
5. I feel obligated to do the right thing.
6. I enjoy giving of my time to others.
7. I am uncomfortable when people talk about emotional issues.
8. I am not uncomfortable when people talk about emotional issues.
9. I don't know what it means to express empathy.
10. I understand what it means to express empathy.
11. I often feel that I miss emotional cues.
12. I pick up emotional cues easily.
13. I have been told that I need to be right.
14. I don't place much value on the need to be right.
15. I seldom talk beyond the surface with friends.
16. My friends and I have deep conversations.
17. I prefer to not be around young children.
18. I love being around young children.
19. I think I tend to take more than I give.
20. I think I tend to give more than I take.
21. I find it easier to show animals affection rather than people.
22. I can give affection to animals and people equally.

23. I have often been called stubborn.
24. I am often told that I am easy to get along with.
25. I prefer to talk more than listen.
26. I prefer to listen more than talk.
27. In most of my conversations I talk more than I listen.
28. In most of my conversations I listen more than I talk.
29. I am uncomfortable getting close to people.
30. I feel comfortable being close to people.

Scoring

Give yourself one point for selecting each of the following statements: 2, 3, 6, 8, 10, 12, 14, 16, 18, 20, 22, 24, 26, 28, and 30.

Subtract one point for selecting each of the following statements: 1, 4, 5, 7, 9, 11, 13, 15, 17, 19, 21, 23, 25, 27, and 29.

Calculate your score.

13–15 points: High empathy

9–12 points: Mild empathy

0–8 points: Low empathy

PERFORMANCE ADDICTION QUESTIONNAIRE

For each question to which you answer yes, circle the statement's number or list the numbers on a separate piece of paper.

1. Did you seldom feel listened to as a child?
2. Did you worry that if you didn't please your parents, you would lose their love?
3. Did you question whether your parents truly loved each other?
4. Did you often feel guilty?
5. Did you seldom have fun with your parents outside of achievement-oriented situations?

6. Were your parents quite concerned with your physical appearance?

7. Were one or both your parents critical people in general?

8. Do you have memories of specific childhood hurts that have never left you?

9. Were you easily humiliated as a young person?

10. Were you considered to be a very sensitive child?

11. Do you believe your past mistakes make you unlovable today?

12. Do you want unconditional acceptance, with no criticism?

13. Do you feel irritated when people close to you are not being capable and efficient?

14. Do you always have a to-do list in your mind or your pocket?

15. Have you considered or have you already had cosmetic surgery?

16. Are you chronically dissatisfied with the way people respond to you?

17. Do you often feel you have to work much harder than others to excel?

18. Do you wonder if anyone really loves anyone else for who they are rather than for what they do?

19. Are you frequently trying to perfect the way you speak?

20. Are you frequently trying to perfect your appearance?

21. Do you often discover that people are far less critical than you imagined?

22. Do you have trouble tolerating your own imperfections?

23. Do you have trouble tolerating others' imperfections?

24. Do you often wonder how much money others make?

25. When friends, relatives, or colleagues have success, do you feel you don't measure up?

26. Are you unable to stop perfectionist thinking even though you know it's irrational?

27. Are you afraid that if you were not so driven, you would be lazy?

28. Do you feel guilty if you just hang out and do nothing?

29. Are you afraid of trying to learn new things for fear of being humiliated?

30. Deep down, do you think you're "not much"?

31. No matter what you think of yourself, do you find that you can't stop thinking about yourself?

32. Does your inner voice tend to be punitive rather than understanding?

33. Do you tend to generalize about yourself in a negative way under stress? (Do you say things to yourself like "I'm so stupid!" or "I'm so fat!"?)

34. Are you seldom content to be with one person in one place for very long?

35. Are you easily bored in conversation?

36. Does your energy pick up when the conversation is about you?

37. Do you like being idealized by others?

38. Do you tend to idealize others?

39. Do you feel pressured to impress others in order to secure their love?

40. Do you fear that loss of status will lead to loss of love?

41. Are you afraid you don't know what true love really is?

42. Have you seldom felt loved the way you want to be loved?

43. Is it difficult for you to truly trust others?

44. Do you question whether you have true friends?

45. Are you afraid your long-term relationship is based on

what you and your partner do for each other rather than a deeper sense of love?

46. Do you have sexual relations infrequently?

47. Are you seldom "present in the moment" during sex?

48. Do you weigh yourself daily?

49. Are you intolerant of weight gain?

50. Are you intolerant of the aging process?

51. Do you imagine if you could perfect certain body parts, your life would be dramatically improved?

52. Do you compare your financial situation to that of others?

53. Do you notice the cars people drive and rate those people accordingly?

54. Do you feel uncomfortable and less worthy in a home that is larger and more extravagant than your own?

55. Do you have a sense of inferiority in relation to people who have more education than you?

56. Do you tend to attach certain personality characteristics to those who attended prestigious schools?

57. Do you rank people according to the affluence of the town or city where they live?

58. Do you feel deprived when a neighbor or friend has a more attractive partner than your own?

59. Do you fantasize about being with someone who is far more attractive than your partner?

60. Do you think that if you were more attractive, you would be with a different partner?

61. Do you think that if you were more successful financially you would be with a different partner?

62. Do you tend to think that other successful people have had unfair advantages?

63. Do you measure another person's success by their social status (money, possessions) to the exclusion of the quality of the person's relationships?

64. Do you measure success without giving much weight to a person's character?
65. Assuming that you know how to care for your body, do you find that you are inconsistent with your self-care measures?
66. Do you exercise too little?
67. Are you on a diet at least once every year?
68. Do you have three or more alcoholic drinks in a single day once a week or more?
69. Do you take sleep aids at least once a month?
70. Do you consider exercise, proper sleep, and good nutrition low priorities in your life?
71. Do you drink more than three caffeinated beverages per day?
72. Do you often eat comfort foods, especially in the evening?
73. Do you seldom think about the quality of your relationships?
74. With each passing year, do you think you become less desirable to others?

Score one point for each question to which you answered yes. Add the total number of points, and use the following scale to rate the level of your performance addiction.

Scoring

60 or more points: Severe performance addiction
50–59 points: Significant performance addiction
40–49 points: Moderate performance addiction
30–39 points: Mild performance addiction
29 or fewer points: Low performance addiction

REINFORCING NEW BELIEFS

It is time to put your newfound insights into practice. First, list the core beliefs that have caused you the most difficulty and stress. Second, describe the typical situations that stimulate each belief. For instance, the false belief "I don't measure up" may be stimulated by the annual performance review process in your workplace. Record the possible consequence attendant on that false belief, such as, "I'll get the lowest raise possible." Test this old view against reality. It is true? Now present the new consequence, based on your new core belief.

False core belief:
Activating event:
Consequence:
Reality check:
New core belief:
New consequence:

FALSE CORE-BELIEF EXERCISE

False core beliefs are usually created in childhood or by several hurtful events later in life. Check the core beliefs that resonate with you. For each one, record in your journal a rational response you have developed. For instance, if you check the statement "I am not competent," you may formulate a rational response such as, "I am not competent in every aspect of my life, but I have certain competencies that are helpful to many people."

CORE BELIEF	RATIONAL RESPONSE
I am unlovable.	
I am less intelligent than most people.	
I am not attractive.	
I don't measure up to other people.	
I panic under stress.	
I am a failure.	
I am not a success.	
I must work harder than others to achieve the same goal.	
Most people don't like me.	
I am not very interesting.	
I have little to offer in a conversation.	
I never seem to have good luck.	
I always get the short end of the stick.	
Bosses always favor my peers more than me.	
I have an ugly body.	
I look old for my age.	
I am always the last person friends confide in.	
I won't be missed if anything happens to me.	
People can't count on me during troubling times.	
People don't feel relaxed when they are with me.	

Now make a list of any additional false core beliefs that you have developed, and follow the same process, formulating a rational response to each one.

Acknowledgments

First of all, I thank the anchors in my life. My wife, Karen, has always expressed her belief in my work, supporting me through the long hours of writing and researching without ever uttering a complaint. Her heart is full of love, and her giving nature allows me to be free to do the work I love. She is the center of our family, and we are all stronger and more resilient because of the love and support she gives so freely.

Our daughter Erica's beautiful spirit and loving ways supported me throughout this process. She is one of those rare individuals who dissipates stress by her mere presence. Her high spirit exudes appreciation of all aspects of life, and her work with the mentally challenged is not only admirable but an example to all of us to appreciate what we have and to be gracious to those who have far less.

I thank our daughter Alaina for always inquiring, "How is the writing going, Dad?" while offering to help in any way I needed. She is not only a fabulous educator but also the most loving, empathic mother any child could ever want. Watching her with our first grand-child, Carmela, brings me joy beyond belief. Her ability to know what Carmela needs, moment to moment, is a supreme example of empathy in action. And Carmela herself is an angel with wings who spreads love every moment of every day to everyone she encounters.

I hope this book will make Carmela's world calmer and less stressful. She and our entire family are all angels in my life.

My son-in-law, Michael, and my son-in-law-to-be, Michael, are both men whom I respect. It gives me great comfort to know that they will always be rocks in our daughters' lives.

My team of supporters — Gerri and Richard Tessicini, Donna and Philip Wood, Diane and Richard Werner, Janice and Jimmy Blackler, Dr. Robert and Maryellen Cherney, and Drs. Valerie Sawyer-Smith and Peter Smith — have encouraged me through the writing of all of my books. I offer grateful thanks for their ongoing faith in my work and most of all for the unreserved love they express to me.

My editor, Jason Gardner, has been a delight to work with from our first phone call. His warm, empathic manner and editorial in-sights are much appreciated. His detailed comments throughout the manuscript were made with unusual thoughtfulness and understand-ing that added needed clarity and flow to the manuscript. I hope we will have the opportunity to work together in the future.

Thanks to my copy editor, Erika Büky, whose meticulous, in-sightful review of the manuscript made this book far more readable than it would have been without her valuable input.

A special, heartfelt thank-you to Yvonne Fantaci for reading every page of the manuscript, making many grammatical correc-tions, and guiding me to define and clarify certain concepts to make the book more reader-friendly.

I thank my good friend Ed Mohebi, CEO of soundmindz.org, for his ongoing faith in my work and for the opportunity to help people throughout the world with state-of-the-art mental health tools and information. I am proud to be a part of such a wonderful venture.

A most grateful thank-you to my clients, whose courage and dedication to exploring and discerning the truth about themselves and our world is a model we should all follow. They have been my best teachers.

Notes

INTRODUCTION

1 "APA Survey Finds Feeling Valued at Work Linked to Well-Being and Performance," press release, American Psychological Association, March 8, 2012, www.apa.org/news/press/releases/2012/03/well-being.aspx.

2 Lydia Saad, "U.S. Workers Least Happy with Their Work Stress and Pay," Gallup, November 12, 2012, www.gallup.com/poll/158723/workers-least -happy-work-stress-pay.aspx.

3 Abiola Keller, Kristin Litzelman, Lauren E. Wisk, Torsheika Maddox, Erika Rose Cheng, Paul D. Creswell, and Whitney P. Witt, "Does the Perception That Stress Affects Health Matter? The Association with Health and Mortality," *Health Psychology* 31, no. 5 (September 2012): 677–84.

4 D. K. Snyder, R. M. Wills, and A. Grady-Fletcher, "Long-Term Effectiveness of Behavioral versus Insight-Oriented Marital Therapy: A Four-Year Follow-Up Study," *Journal of Consulting and Clinical Psychology* 59 (1991): 138–41. Katty Coffron, "Does Couple Therapy Really Work: Helping You to Live and Love Well," December 23, 2013, http://pasoroblesmarriage counseling.com/does-couple-therapy-really-work/.

CHAPTER 1. WHY *YOU* SHOULD CARE ABOUT STRESS

1   "Stress at Work," Centers for Disease Control and Prevention, www.cdc
     .gov/niosh/topics/stress, accessed January 20, 2016.
2   N. Anderson, C. D. Belar, S. Breckler, K. Nordal, D. W. Ballard, L. F.
     Bufka, L. Bossolo, S. Behurne, A. Brownawell, and K. Wiggins, "Stress in
     America," press release, American Psychological Association, February 4,
     2015, www.apa.org/news/press/releases/stress/2014/stress-report.pdf.
3   "American Psychological Association Survey Shows Money Stress Weigh-
     ing on Americans' Health Nationwide," press release, American Psycho-
     logical Association, February 4, 2015, www.apa.org/news/press/releases
     /2015/02/money-stress.aspx.
4   H. Gotlib, J. LeMoult, N. L. Colich, L. C. Foland-Ross, J. Hallmayer, J.
     Joormann, J. Lin, and O. M. Wolkowitz, "Telomere Length and Cortisol Re-
     activity in Children of Depressed Mothers," *Molecular Psychiatry* 20 (2015):
     615–20, www.nature.com/mp/journal/v20/n5/full/mp2014119a.html.
5   Premal H. Thaker, Liz Y. Han, Aparna A. Kamat, Jesusa M. Arevalo, Rie
     Takahashi, Chunhua Lu, Nicholas B. Jennings, Guillermo Armaiz-Pena,
     James A. Bankson, Murali Ravoori, William M. Merritt, Yvonne G. Lin,
     Lingegowda S. Mangala, Tae Jin Kim, Robert L. Coleman, Charles N.
     Landen, Yang Li, Edward Felix, Angela M. Sanguino, Robert A. Newman,
     Mary Lloyd, David M. Gershenson, Vikas Kundra, Gabriel Lopez-Berestein,
     Susan K. Lutgendorf, Steven W. Cole, and Anil K. Sood, "Chronic Stress
     Promotes Tumor Growth and Angiogenesis in a Mouse Model of Ovarian
     Carcinoma, *Nature Medicine* 12 (2006): 939–44, doi:10.1038/nm1447.
6   Shana Lynch, "Why Your Workplace Might Be Killing You," Insights by
     Stanford Business, February 23, 2015, www.gsb.stanford.edu/insights
     /why-your-workplace-might-be-killing-you.
7   George Jucket, "Mental Disorders due to Permanent Stress," *Science Daily*,
     November 21, 2014, www.sciencedaily.com/releases/2014/11/141121082907.
     htm.
8   Monika Fleshner, Stephen F. Maier, David M. Lyons, and Murray C.
     Raskind, "The Neurobiology of the Stress-Resistant Brain," *Stress* 14, no. 5
     (2011), http://dx.doi.org/10.3109%2F10253890.2011.596865.

CHAPTER 2. EXPANDING OUR HUMANITY:
THE DISCIPLINE OF EMPATHY

1   Daniel Goleman, *Emotional Intelligence: Why It Can Matter More Than IQ*
     (New York: Bantam, 1995), 103–4. Also, L. Brothers, "A Biological Per-
     spective on Empathy," *American Journal of Psychiatry* 146 (1989), 1.

2   Kira Birditt, Nicky Newton, James Cranford, and Lindsay Ryan, "Stress and Negative Relationship Quality among Older Couples: Implications for Blood Pressure," *Journals of Gerontology, Series B* (April 2015), http://psychsocgerontology.oxfordjournals.org/content/early/2015/04/06/geronb.gbv023.abstract.

3   W. Redford and V. Parrot Williams, *Anger Kills* (New York: HarperCollins, 1994).

4   Tomas Charmorro-Premuzic, "Can You Really Improve Your Emotional Intelligence?" *Harvard Business Review*, May 29, 2013, https://hbr.org/2013/05/can-you-really-improve-your-em.

CHAPTER 3. EMPATHIC LISTENING: LOVING AWAY STRESS

1   "Mayo Clinic Research: Broken Heart Syndrome," *Sonoran Living*, February 14, 2014, www.youtube.com/watch?v=5f2Ga5O55k8.

2   Quoted in Frederick Brussat and Mary Ellen Brussat, *Spiritual Literacy: Reading the Sacred in Everyday Life* (New York: Scribner, 1996), 283.

CHAPTER 4. THE SOUL'S PHARMACY: HOW TO PRODUCE CALMING NEUROCHEMICALS

1   Daniel J. Siegel, *The Developing Mind: Toward a Neurobiology of Interpersonal Experience*, 2nd ed. (New York: Guilford, 2015).

2   George E. Vaillant, *Triumphs of Experience: The Men of the Harvard Grant Study* (Cambridge, MA: Harvard University Press, 2012).

3   "Brain Scan Can Predict Who Responds Best to Certain Treatment for Obsessive-Compulsive Disorder," press release, UCLA newsroom, June 23, 2015, http://newsroom.ucla.edu/releases/brain-scan-can-predict-who-responds-best-to-certain-treatment-for-obsessive-compulsive-disorder.

CHAPTER 6. CBT IN ACTION: COMBATING THE DISTORTIONS OF PERSONALIZATION AND BLAME

1   Judith Lynn Fisher-Blando, "Workplace Bullying: Aggressive Behavior and Its Effect on Job Satisfaction and Productivity" (PhD diss., University of Phoenix, 2008).

2   Workplace Bullying Institute, U.S. Workplace Bullying Survey, February 2014, workplacebullying.org.

3   Irving L. Janis, *Groupthink: Psychological Studies of Policy Decisions and Fiascoes*, 2nd ed. (Boston: Wadsworth, 1982).

CHAPTER 7. CBT IN ACTION: COMBATING NEGATIVE SELF-TALK AND ENDING THE CYCLE OF STRESS

1   E. Kross, E. Bruehlman-Senecal, J. Park, A. Burson, A. Dougherty, H. Shablack, R. Bremner, J. Moser, and O. Ayduk, "Self-Talk as a Regulatory Mechanism: How You Do It Matters," *Journal of Personality and Social Psychology* 106, no. 2 (2014): 304–24, http://selfcontrol.psych.lsa.umich.edu /wp-content/uploads/2014/01/KrossJ_Pers_Soc_Psychol2014Self-talk _as_a_regulatory_mechanism_How_you_do_it_matters.pdf.

2   A. Hatzigeorgiadis, N. Zourbanos, E. Galanis, and Y. Theodorakis, "Self-Talk and Sports Performance: A Meta-analysis," *Perspectives on Psychological Science* 6, no. 4 (July 2011): 348–56.

3   S. G. Rogelberg, L. Justice, P. W. Braddy, S. C. Paustian-Underdahl, E. Heggestad, L. Shanock, B. E. Baran, et al., "The Executive Mind: Leader Self-Talk, Effectiveness and Strain," *Journal of Managerial Psychology* 28, no. 2 (2013), www.emeraldinsight.com/action/doSearch?ContribStored =Rogelberg%2C+S+G.

CHAPTER 8. CBT IN ACTION: COMBATING PERFORMANCE ADDICTION

1   William Ickes, *Empathic Accuracy* (New York: Guilford,1997).

CHAPTER 9. CLEAR EYES: PERCEIVING THE TRUTH THROUGH EMPATHY, NOT PREJUDICE

1   D. Sussman, "Negative View of U.S. Race Relations Grows, Poll Finds," *New York Times*, May 4, 2015, www.nytimes.com/2015/05/05/us/negative -view-of-us-race-relations-grows-poll-finds.html?_r=0.

2   "Familiarity Breeds Empathy," *UQ News*, May 8, 2015, www.uq.edu.au /news/article/2015/05/familiarity-breeds-empathy.

3   "Prejudice Comes from a Basic Human Need and Way of Thinking, New Research Suggests," *Science Daily*, December 21, 2011, www.sciencedaily .com/releases/2011/12/111221140627.htm.

CHAPTER 11. EMPATHY, SELF-CARE, AND WELL-BEING

1   World Health Organization, *Health Topics: Obesity*, www.who.int/topics /obesity/en, accessed January 20, 2016.

2 M. A. B. Veldhorst, G. Noppe, M. H. T. M. Jongejan, C. B. M. Kok, S. Mekic, J. W. Koper, E. F. C. van Rossum, and E. L. T. van den Akker, "Increased Scalp Hair Cortisol Concentration in Obese Children," *Journal of Clinical Endocrinology and Metabolism* 99 (December 2013), http://press .endocrine.org/doi/10.1210/jc.2013-2924.

3 Silva U. Maier, Aidan B. Makwana, and Todd A. Hare, "Acute Stress Impairs Self-Control in Goal-Directed Choice by Altering Multiple Functional Connections within the Brain's Decision Circuits," *Neuron* 87, no. 3 (August 2015): 621–31, http://dx.doi.org/10.1016/j.neuron.2015.07.005.

4 Premysl Bercik, Emmanuel Denou, Josh Collins, Wendy Jackson, Jun Lu, Jennifer Jury, Yikang Deng, et al., "The Intestinal Microbiota Affect Central Levels of Brain-Derived Neurotropic Factor and Behavior in Mice," *Gastroenterology* 141, no. 2 (August 2011): 599–609.

5 Emmy Werner, *Through the Eyes of Innocents* (New York: Basic Books, 2001).

6 Paul Zak, "Trust, Morality — and Oxytocin?" presentation at TEDGlobal 2011, July 2011, www.ted.com/talks/paul_zak_trust_morality_and_oxytocin.

7 L. J. Martin, G. Hathaway, K. Isbester, S. Mirali, E. L. Acland, N. Niederstrasser, P. M. Slepian, et al., "Reducing Social Stress Elicits Emotional Contagion of Pain in Mouse and Human Strangers," *Current Biology* 25, no. 3 (February 2015): 326–32, http://dx.doi.org/10.1016/j.cub.2014.11.028.

8 Gretchen Reynolds, "The Right Dose of Exercise for a Longer Life," *New York Times,* April 15, 2015, well.blogs.nytimes.com/2015/04/15/the-right -dose-of-exercise-for-a-longer-life.

9 Edward F. Coyle, "Very Intense Exercise Training Is Extremely Potent and Time Efficient: A Reminder," *Journal of Applied Physiology* 98, no. 6 (2005): 1983–84.

10 Nico S. Rizzo, Karen Jaceldo-Siegl, Joan Sabate, and Gary E. Fraser, "Nutrient Profiles of Vegetarian and Nonvegetarian Dietary Patterns," *Journal of the Academy of Nutrition and Dietetics* 113, no. 12 (December 2013): 1610–19, http://dx.doi.org/10.1016/j.jand.2013.06.349.

11 C. M. Depner, M. G. Traber, G. Bobe, E. Kensicki, K. M. Bohren, G. Milne, and D. B. Jump, "Metabolomic Analysis of Omega-3 Fatty Acid-Mediated Attenuation of Western Diet-Induced Nonalcoholic Steatohepatitis in LDLR-/- Mice," *PLOS One*, December 17, 2013, http://journals.plos .org/plosone/article?id=10.1371/journal.pone.0083756.

12 S. A. Johnson, A. Figueroa, N. Navaei, A. Wong, R. Kalfon, L. T.

Ormsbee, R. G. Feresin, et al., "Daily Blueberry Consumption Improves Blood Pressure and Arterial Stiffness in Postmenopausal Women with Pre- and Stage 1 Hypertension: A Randomized, Double-Blind, Placebo-Controlled Clinical Trial," *Journal of the Academy of Nutrition and Dietetics* 115, no. 3 (March 2015): 369–77, http://www.sciencedirect.com/science/article/pii/S2212267214016335.

13   Elizabeth Renter, "Chamomile Shown to Battle Anxiety, Depression Significantly," Natural Society, September 5, 2013, http://naturalsociety.com/chamomile-reduc-anxiety-depression.

CHAPTER 12. "GIVE AND YOU SHALL RECEIVE": HOW GIVING AND GOODNESS RESTORE CALM

1   William Brown, Nathan Considine, and Carol Magai, "Altruism Relates to Health in an Ethnically Diverse Sample of Older Adults," *Journals of Gerontology, Series B* 60, no. 3 (May 2005): 143–52.

2   P. Wink and M. Dillon, "Spiritual Development across the Adult Life Course: Findings from a Longitudinal Study," *Journal of Adult Development* 9, no. 1 (January 2002): 79–94.

3   Charles Darwin, *The Descent of Man and Selection in Relation to Sex* (London: John Murray, 1871), chapter 4.

4   Alan Luks and Peggy Payne, *The Healing Power of Doing Good* (New York: Fawcett Columbine, 1992).

5   Michael J. Poulin, Stephanie L. Brown, Amanda J. Dillard, and Dylan M. Smith, "Giving to Others and the Association between Stress and Mortality," *American Journal of Public Health* 103, no. 9 (September 2013): 1649–55, http://doi. 10.2105/AJPH.2012.300876.

6   Maureen Salamon, "11 Interesting Effects of Oxytocin," *Live Science*, December 3, 2010, http://www.livescience.com/35219-11-effects-of-oxytocin.html.

7   R. D. Enright and R. P. Fitzgibbons, *Forgiveness Therapy* (Washington, DC: American Psychological Association, 2014).

8   His Holiness the Dalai Lama and Howard C. Cutler, "Inner Happiness, Outer Happiness and Trust," chapter 12 in *The Art of Happiness in a Troubled World* (New York: Doubleday Religion, 2009), 247–51.

9   P. Levine and M. Kline, *Trauma through a Child's Eyes* (Berkeley, CA: North Atlantic Books, 2007).

10   Richard Tedeschi and Lawrence Calhoun, "Tempered by Fire," *Psychology Today*, September 24, 2013.

CHAPTER 13. I AM WHO I AM:
HOW AUTHENTICITY SOOTHES THE SOUL

1   J. Brennan, *The Art of Becoming Oneself* (Tarentum, PA: Word Association Publishers, 2011).

2   Abigail A. Mengers, "The Benefits of Being Yourself: An Examination of Authenticity, Uniqueness, and Well-Being" (PhD diss., University of Pennsylvania, 2014).

Recommended Reading

Begley, Sharon. *Train Your Mind, Change Your Brain*. New York: Ballantine, 2007.

Brennan, J. *The Art of Becoming Oneself*. Tarentum, PA: Word Association, 2011.

Buettner, Dan. *The Blue Zones: Lessons for Living Longer from the People Who've Lived the Longest*. Washington, DC: National Geographic Society, 2008.

Campbell, T. Colin. *The China Study*. Dallas: Benbella Books, 2006.

Cayoun, B. A. *Mindfulness Integrated CBT for Well-Being and Personal Growth: Four Steps to Enhance Inner Calm, Self-Confidence and Relationships*. West Sussex, UK: Wiley Blackwell, 2015.

Chödrön, Pema. *The Places That Scare Us: A Guide to Fearlessness in Difficult Times*. Boston: Shambhala, 2002.

Ciaramicoli, Arthur. *Changing Your Inner Voice: A Journey through Depression to Truth and Love*. Raleigh, NC: Lulu, 2012.

———. *Performance Addiction: The Dangerous New Syndrome and How to Stop It from Ruining Your Life*. Hoboken, NJ: Wiley, 2004.

———. *Transforming Anxiety into Joy: A Practical Workbook to Gain Emotional Freedom*. Raleigh, NC: Lulu, 2012.

————. *Treatment of Abuse and Addiction: A Holistic Approach*. Northvale, NJ: Jason Aronson, 1997.

Ciaramicoli, Arthur, and Katherine Ketcham. *The Power of Empathy: A Practical Guide to Creating Intimacy, Self-Understanding, and Lasting Love*. New York: Plume, 2001.

Ciaramicoli, Arthur, with John Allen Mollenhauer, *The Curse of the Capable: The Hidden Challenges to a Balanced, Healthy, High-Achieving Life*. Garden City, NY: Morgan James, 2010.

DeWaal, Frans. *The Age of Empathy: Nature's Lessons for a Kindred Society*. New York: Three Rivers, 2009.

Emmons, Robert. *Thanks: How Practicing Gratitude Can Make You Happy*. New York: Houghton Mifflin, 2007.

Gilbert, Daniel. *Stumbling on Happiness*. New York: Vintage Books, 2007.

Hanh, Thich Nhat. *True Love: A Practice for Awakening the Heart*. Boston: Shambhala, 2011.

Kahneman, Daniel. *Thinking, Fast and Slow*. New York: Farrar, Straus and Giroux, 2013.

Klein, Stefan. *The Science of Happiness*. New York: Marlowe, 2002.

Kolts, Rand, and T. Chodron. *An Open-Hearted Life*. Boston: Shambhala, 2015.

Merzenich, Michael. *Soft-Wired: How the New Science of Brain Plasticity Can Change Your Life*. San Francisco: Parnassus, 2013.

Pausch, Randy. *The Last Lecture*. New York: Hyperion, 2008.

Pelletier, Kenneth. *Sound Mind, Sound Body: A New Model for Lifelong Health*. New York: Fireside, 1994.

Ratey, John. *Spark: The Revolutionary New Science of Exercise and the Brain*. New York: Little, Brown, 2008.

Rifkin, Jeremy. *The Empathic Civilization: The Race to Global Consciousness in a World in Crisis*. New York: Penguin, 2009.

Rohr, Richard. *Falling Upward: A Spirituality for the Two Halves of Life*. New York: Jossey-Bass, 2011.

————. *Simplicity: The Freedom of Letting Go*. New York: Crossroad, 2003.

Schreiber-Servan, David. *Anti-cancer: A New Way of Life*. New York: Viking, 2008.

Szalavitz, Maia, and Bruce Perry. *Born for Love: Why Empathy Is Essential and Endangered*. New York: William Morrow, 2010.

Index

About the Author

A rthur P. Ciaramicoli, EdD, PhD, is a licensed clinical psychologist who has been treating clients for more than thirty-five years. He is a member of the American Psychological Association and the Massachusetts Psychological Association.

Dr. Ciaramicoli is the chief medical officer of soundmindz.org. He has been on the faculty of Harvard Medical School for several years, lecturer for the American Cancer Society, chief psychologist at Metrowest Medical Center, and director of the Metrowest Counseling Center and of the alternative medicine division of Metrowest Wellness Center in Framingham, Massachusetts.

Dr. Ciaramicoli has lectured at Harvard Health Services, Boston College Counseling Center, and the Space Telescope Science Institute in Baltimore as well as serving as a consultant to several major corporations in the Boston area.

Dr. Ciaramicoli has appeared on CNN, CNNfn, Fox News Boston, Comcast TV, New England Cable News, *Good Morning*

America Weekend, The O'Reilly Report, and other shows. He has been a weekly radio guest on *Your Healthy Family* on Sirius Satellite Radio and *Holistic Health Today,* and he has been interviewed on *The People's Pharmacy, The Gary Null Show,* and more than two dozen other radio programs airing on NPR, XM Radio, and numerous AM and FM stations.

Dr. Ciaramicoli is the author of *The Curse of the Capable: The Hidden Challenges to a Balanced, Healthy, High Achieving Life* (Wiley, 2010), *Performance Addiction: The Dangerous New Syndrome and How to Stop It from Ruining Your Life* (Wiley, 2004), and *The Power of Empathy: A Practical Guide to Creating Intimacy, Self-Understanding, and Lasting Love* (Dutton, 2000), which has been published in seven languages. His first book, *Treatment of Abuse and Addiction: A Holistic Approach* (Jason Aronson, 1997), was selected as Book of the Month by *Psychotherapy Book News.* He is also the coauthor of *Beyond the Influence: Understanding and Defeating Alcoholism* (Bantam, 2000) and founder of the Empathy and Goodness Project on Facebook and Healthy Empathic Achievement on LinkedIn.

He has also authored the apps Anti-Anxiety and Anti-Depression and two workbooks in collaboration with soundmindz.org: *Transforming Anxiety into Joy: A Practical Workbook to Gain Emotional Freedom* (2012) and *Changing Your Inner Voice: A Journey through Depression to Truth and Love* (2012).

Dr. Ciaramicoli lives in a suburb of Boston with his wife of thirty-five years. His website is www.balanceyoursuccess.com. His Twitter handle is docapc.